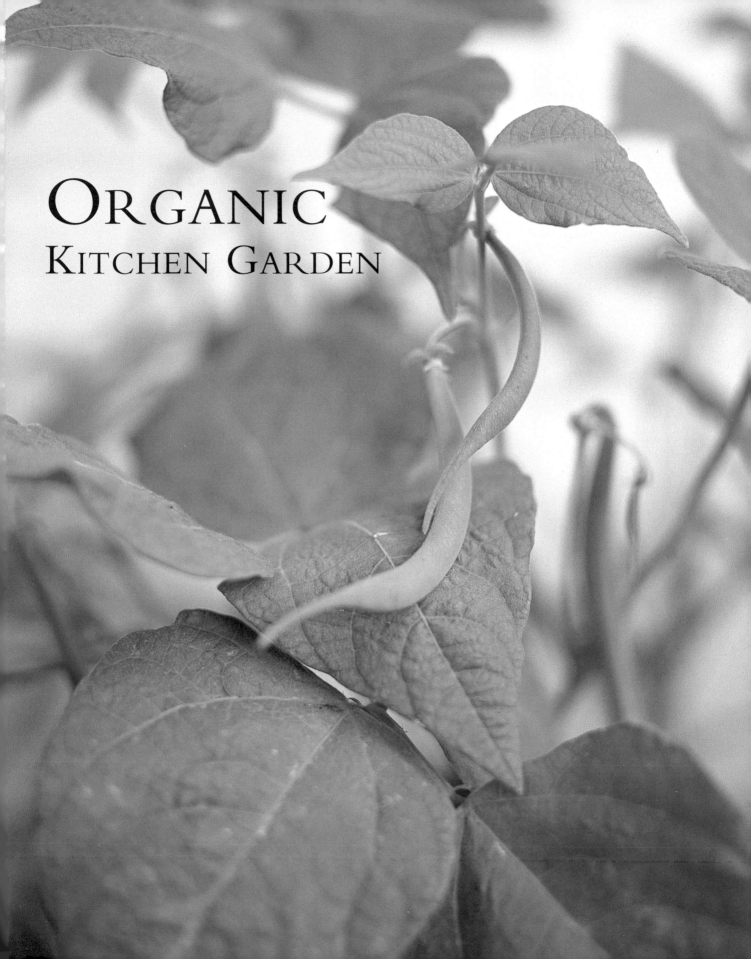

ORGANIC
KITCHEN GARDEN

THE
ORGANIC
GARDENING
CATALOGUE

ORGANICALLY GROWN SEEDS, ORGANIC

VEGETABLE SEEDS

PEA

DOUCE PROVENCE

HEIGHT 2ft.

GARDENS
ILLUSTRATED

PHOTOGRAPHS BY Gavin Kingcome

juliet roberts

ORGANIC
KITCHEN GARDEN

conran OCTOPUS

contents

history

Audley End's historic kitchen garden fell into
decline after two World Wars irrevocably changed Britain's
social climate. It has now been restored to its former glory
in a unique collaboration between English Heritage
and the Henry Doubleday Research Association (HDRA).

OPPOSITE Head Kitchen Gardener Mike Thurlow believes there's
a tomato to suit pretty much everyone's taste and each year
enjoys experimenting with many different sorts. He grows
more than fifty different varieties, including plum tomatoes,
in the restored glasshouse and around the walled garden.

Traditional walled kitchen gardens have a particular magic. They seem to resonate with memories of a bygone age when every country estate employed a team of skilled gardeners to serve the household with top quality fruit, vegetables and flowers all year round. The walled, one-hectare (two-acre) kitchen garden at Audley End in Essex is a particularly fine example, and has been sensitively restored in a unique collaboration between English Heritage and the Henry Doubleday Research Association (HDRA) – Europe's largest organic gardening organization. Work began on the overgrown and semi-derelict garden on 1 January 1999, and the garden was opened just three months later. The project has proved a huge success and the immaculate, neat beds are once again yielding fine vegetables, fruit and flowers throughout the year.

The kitchen garden at Audley End dates back to the 1750s, and was originally known as Lady Portsmouth's garden, after its owner. The original

2.7m- (9ft-) high brick walls that enclose the garden form a sheltered microclimate, which skilled head gardeners down the years have used to aid productivity. Alterations during the 19th century included a vine-house along the south-facing wall and an orchard house in the centre of the garden.

Kitchen gardens reached their productive peak in Victorian times: the result of cheap manual labour, strict social hierarchy and advances in science and technology. But the social climate changed irrevocably after the male population was decimated by two world wars and – hastened by the rise in market gardens – many kitchen gardens fell into decline. Audley End was no exception. During the Second World War, the house and grounds served as the headquarters of the Polish section of the Special Operations Executive, then in 1948 the property was purchased by the Ministry of Works, the predecessor to English Heritage.

However, unlike many of its counterparts, which invariably became sad, bramble-filled ruins, Audley End's kitchen garden was kept ticking over by a market garden company. After the market gardeners retired in 1998, English Heritage established a programme to return the kitchen garden to its former glory. Unlike other restoration projects that attempt to recreate a facsimile of the past, English Heritage took the unprecedented step of collaborating with HDRA. Their aim was to make Audley End a centre of excellence that would marry the best Victorian horticultural practices with modern organic methods. This might at first seem rather an odd combination – as Victorian gardeners were renowed for using noxious chemicals – however, they were skilled at looking after the soil which, as Mike Thurlow, Audley End's head kitchen gardener explains, 'is the very cornerstone of the organic movement'.

Mike, who started gardening 'at his grandfather's heels', trained at Usk College in Gwent and has worked at Dyffryn Gardens, Aberglasney, and Barnsdale Gardens, Rutland. He recalls putting his head around the door of the garden at Audley End for the first time back in 1999: 'It was just a muddy strip, but I was so excited. It was the perfect opportunity for me to combine my interest in gardening history with my skills as an organic gardener.'

The first tasks were to establish the layout of the garden, install the permanent planting and cultivate the soil. During the initial months of the project, while the earth was scraped out to allow the onsite archaeologist to uncover the original path system laid in the 1700s, Mike researched fruit trees and drew up plant lists. December was rather late to be ordering bare-root specimens, but by good fortune he managed to obtain all the varieties he needed. 'It was important to get the fruit trees and bushes in as soon as we could so that they could build up their fruiting wood,' explains Mike.

BELOW In true Victorian fashion, the garden is kept immaculately neat and tidy. OPPOSITE One of the first tasks of the restoration team was to rebuild the gardens' traditional hoggin pathways and edge them with more than a mile of box hedging.

history

The garden at Audley End is divided into four main compartments, around which espalier and other trained fruits have been established; an orchard house sits at the centre of the plot and the restored vinery extends across the south-facing wall. The main paths around the garden were rebuilt with traditional hoggin, and Mike ordered more than a mile of box hedging to line the edges. To the south of the orchard house the land is entirely dedicated to the main vegetable production and is subdivided into quarters, which fits in rather conveniently with Mike's four-year crop rotation system.

The inner walls of the garden are lined with fruit trees, with their locations dictated by the prevailing conditions. Alongside a permanent asparagus bed, soft fruit bushes such as raspberries, currants and gooseberries, as well as strawberries and cut flowers, are grown in the area between the vinery and the orchard house. Behind the vinery there is a row of buildings including the old boiler house, the under-gardener's

bothy, the potting shed, the tool store and forcing house. These buildings look out on to the 21st Century Garden, which is currently being developed to display the modern methods used in organic gardening.

Fortunately the soil at Audley End is wonderfully rich, having been carefully maintained for hundreds of years. In order to meet the historical requirements

LEFT Soft fruit bushes, such as these raspberries, are grown in the area between the vinery and the orchard house.
ABOVE Mike grows an abundance of flowers not only for their sheer beauty, but to encourage beneficial insects such as bees, ladybirds and lacewings into the garden.

Heritage seed library border

Herbaceous Perennials

Seakale ~ Rhubarb ~ Jerusalem artichoke etc.

Dahlias

BED 1

BED 2

ORCHARD HOUSE

Asparagus bed

Raspberries

Early Veg.

VINE HOUSES

BED 4

BED 3

Chrysanths Annuals Sweet Peas BED 1

Currants & Gooseberries

Strawberries BED 3

Artichokes BED 2

Early Veg

LODGE

Well

Herbaceous Perennials

Vegetables

Herbs

→ N

set by English Heritage, Mike uses mostly Victorian varieties of vegetables or varieties that were available up to the 1900s. 'I get enormous satisfaction knowing that a Victorian gardener would have been familiar with ninety per cent of the types that we grow here,' he smiles. Mike finds that the pest and disease resistance of the older varieties is very often every bit as good as that of their modern counterparts and, by using organic practices and working with nature, he has proved again and again that most problems can be dealt with effectively.

The authenticity of the restoration of the kitchen garden at Audley End has been helped greatly by the timely discovery of a detailed diary that belonged to a journeyman gardener, William Cresswell, who worked at the garden in 1874. His handwritten account of the running of the kitchen garden, together with some

handy anecdotes from the Right Honourable Mrs Catherine Ruck, who lived in the house up until the Second World War, have been invaluable. Mike has a facsimile of the original diary and takes great pleasure in comparing notes.

Mike works alongside three full-time gardeners and a team of volunteers. 'The garden quickly made the transition from a restoration programme to a proper working garden,' he says with satisfaction. 'The paths have developed a personality and the fruit trees are establishing nicely.'

The hard work and dedication of the team responsible for Audley End's remarkable restoration have come to fruition: walking through the strong wooden door set in the 18th-century brick walls is as close as it is now possible to get to the heyday of horticultural excellence.

ABOVE The garden is divided into four main compartments, which are subdivided into vegetable growing areas, and beds for perennials crops, soft fruit and flowers. The orchard house sits in the centre and the vinery across the south facing wall.

kitchen garden basics

PLANNING THE VEGETABLE GARDEN

'For the Victorians, kitchen gardening was all about extending the seasons and getting the most out of your plot,' explains Mike. 'A considered layout, careful planning, successional sowing and good gardening practices were of paramount importance. If a crop failed there was no such thing as nipping out and getting something from the shops!' To help him plan the year ahead, Mike plots out the week-by-week tasks in a big diary. As the year passes he also records what he has planted, cropping seasons and the results of the harvests. 'I don't always stick to it, but it helps me focus my priorities and avoid bottle-necks in the workload,' he says.

ASSESSING THE PLOT

Whatever the size of your plot – whether it is a walled kitchen garden, an allotment or a section of a back garden – Mike advises taking your time in getting to know your plot and planning the optimum layout. What is the orientation? Which direction is the prevailing wind? Are there any frost pockets? Which areas are warmest and coolest? What, if any, protection is there? Are there any trees that will cast shade and be greedy with water? Is there a source of water?

'The text-book perfect plot would be south-facing on a slight incline with well-drained, rich loamy soil,' Mike says. 'But very few gardens fit this description and it is important to assess the pros and cons and to work them to your best advantage.' He suggests staggering cropping times by using the sunny and shady areas in the garden to help advance crops or hold them back, and benefiting from the drier/wetter spots in the garden to grow plants that thrive in those particular conditions.

It is useful to find out exactly what sort of soil you are dealing with. Dig a hole 60cm (2ft) deep and see if water drains into it. It's also worth buying a kit to find out the pH value and getting your soil analysed. 'To grow veg, a pH of 7–7.5 is ideal,' says Mike. 'Find out what your neighbours are growing and ask them what does well. Each area has its own particular qualities, and it's worth taking into account and building on other people's knowledge of the locality. When I began at Audley End I wanted it to be a botanic garden of vegetables, then I realized that out of, say, 25 varieties maybe only six will do really well.'

ABOVE The vinery runs along the south-facing wall and thus is exposed to maximum sunlight; the brick walls are lined with a variety of fruit trees whose locations are dicated by the prevailing conditions.
OPPOSITE Table showing the four-year crop rotation at Audley End.

AUDLEY END'S FOUR-YEAR CROP ROTATION

	YEAR 1	YEAR 2	YEAR 3	YEAR 4
BED 1	Root crops	Potatoes	Legumes	Brassicas
BED 2	Brassicas	Root crops	Potatoes	Legumes
BED 3	Legumes	Brassicas	Root crops	Potatoes
BED 4	Potatoes	Legumes	Brassicas	Root crops

ORIENTATION

A simple, but effective way to improve your chances of success is to arrange rows so that they get maximum exposure to the sun. If possible, rows should run north–south, so that as the sun makes its daily round it shines first on the east side then moves over the top of the rows to the west. If rows run east–west, the north-facing side of crops gets little sun, which can be particularly detrimental for taller crops.

PLANNING WHAT TO GROW

Regulating the quantity, variety and supply of crops to meet your needs is one of the main stumbling blocks. Mike suggests thinking about what crops you most like eating and making a list of the estimated quantities of individual vegetables required and when they are in season. 'Try to assess the return you'll get from the space available,' he says. If ground is at a premium he advises growing things that will make good use of space such as beans, perpetual spinach (which tends not to bolt so readily as ordinary spinach), onions, leeks, and cut-and-come-again lettuces. These can be interspersed with catch crops that grow in a short season, such as radish, beetroot, turnips and kohlrabi.

The key to avoiding gluts of certain vegetables is to sow seed little and often – known as successional sowing. This is particularly important with crops that are quick to mature, such as radish and lettuce.

Catch cropping and intercropping also ensure the best use of the ground. They are similar in that they take advantage of fast-maturing crops: a catch crop is grown on the land that has a free period between the harvest of an early crop and planting out of a later one; intercropping is the practice of growing a fast-maturing crop between the rows of slower growing crops.

CROP ROTATION

Mike practises a four-year crop rotation system in the kitchen garden (see table, above) so that the main vegetable groups (root crops, potatoes, legumes and brassicas) are moved through the four main beds. This not only helps prevent the build up of pests and diseases in the soil but also ensures that as different crops make different demands upon the soil, the nutrients available are used more efficiently. Vegetables that do not fit into these categories, such as beetroot and sweetcorn, can be used as gap fillers around the garden.

SOIL

Digging the soil over loosens any compaction and allows you to remove any large bricks or stones hidden beneath the surface. 'We remove all stones over about 5cm (2in) big, but it's a good idea to leave the smaller ones as they create cool areas,' says Mike. He advises single digging, using a spade to take out a trench, then driving a fork into the bottom of the trench to break up any compact earth.

'It helps open up the soil so that rain can get through and plants can draw on reserves below,' explains Mike. Dig organic matter into the trench, as required, and then replace the topsoil.

IMPROVING THE SOIL

Well-rotted manure and homemade compost are both excellent soil conditioners, but being rather smelly can prove problematic for town gardeners. Mike suggests contacting your local council to check the availability of recycled green waste from parks and urban landscaping. Your organic matter can either be incorporated into the soil when single digging or spread across the surface of the soil and forked in. As an additional way to boost growth, Mike sprinkles the soil's surface with pelleted chicken manure, and waters plants with dilute liquid seaweed fertilizer.

GREEN MANURES

A further method of improving soil fertility and structure is to grow green manures (also known as cover crops) and incorporate them into the soil by digging in. Mike sows over-wintering varieties such as Italian and Hungarian rye grass in late summer/autumn as well as early March. 'They are a good way of bulking up the soil and their fibrous roots help bind the earth together,' he explains. Acting rather like a blanket, green manures keep down the soil's moisture content, which in turn means the earth will warm up quicker in spring. They also help protect the soil and lock in nutrients that the winter rains would otherwise wash away. Mike sows clover and tares any time from April until the end of September, as they prefer warmer conditions to germinate. These varieties lock nitrogen into the soil and are particularly useful in areas where you intend to grow nitrogen-hungry plants such as brassicas.

'It's worth targeting a different plot around the garden each year and always bear in mind that it has to be dug in, so don't over commit yourself by planting

1 Italian and Hungarian rye grass makes ideal green manures. 2 Mike broadcast sows seed at a rate of roughly 30g per square metre. 3 This is then raked in. 4 Dig in green manures two to three weeks before the land is needed. 5 Flip green side over and chop with a spade to break up.

too big an area,' Mike suggests. The seed should be broadcast evenly at a rate of around 30g/sq m (1oz/sq yd) – roughly half of that used for a lawn – and lightly raked in. Mike digs the green manure in two to three weeks before he wants to use the land to allow the nitrogen to be released and the 'sting' to go out of it before planting. 'To incorporate it back into the soil simply dig to a spade's depth and flip it over: green side down, and roots up, the chop in to it slightly to break it up.' If the green manure has grown long, he mows it down and uses the clippings for the compost heap.

MULCHING

After the winter rains, mulching the soil helps to conserve the available moisture and also helps suppress weeds. A mulch can consist of organic matter, such as grass clippings, straw or compost, which will rot into the soil over time, or inorganic material such as black plastic, old carpet or even grit and stone. Mike also creates a 'dry mulch' by hoeing the soil and loosening up the top layer. Mulches can help insulate the soil and reduce the need to cultivate.

SOWING SEED

It's a good idea to start every year with fresh seed and compost. New trays and pots are sterile, but if you are reusing last year's then give them a thorough scrub. For seed sowing he uses a variety of different-sized pots, modules and rigid seed trays, which will not twist and turn and so damage the roots. He is also careful to use environmentally friendly products. 'Getting rid of broken plastic flower pots is a big problem, so we always use biodegradable plastics, which usually last a couple

of seasons.' For planting on, Mike uses the Victorian terracotta pots discovered during the restoration of Audley End. 'There were over 5,000 of them stacked against a wall and they've been a real godsend,' he says.

COMPOST

Mike recommends experimenting with different brands of non-peat-based compost, then sticking to your favourite. 'Always use seed-sowing compost to start your seeds off rather than a general compost. Seed-sowing compost has low fertility, good drainage and a fine texture,' he says. 'General compost has a slightly coarser nature and much higher level of nutrients and although seeds will germinate in it the young roots tend to get burnt off. It's much better suited for potting on.'

SOWING SEED UNDER GLASS

To gain a few extra weeks' growth at the start of the season Mike sows frost-tender crops under the protection of a greenhouse or cloche. However, it is worth noting that some crops do not respond well to having their roots disturbed by transplanting and do better if grown in situ on soil warmed by fleece or cloches. Alternatively, grow in individual modules to limit root disturbance. To give young plants a good start in life, Mike advises watering drills and planting holes with dilute liquid fertilizer prior to transplanting or sowing.

SOWING IN SITU

Although seed packets often recommend sowing outdoors as early as February, Mike believes that starting too early often leads to disappointment and believes in letting the weather be his guide. Early in the year he regularly tests the ground with a soil thermometer

LEFT To help extend the growing season, Mike uses traditional chase barn cloches to warm the soil prior to planting in the early part of the year. Tender young plants grown in situ also benefit from the protecion of either cloches or horticultural fleece.

kitchen garden basics

first thing in the morning, pushing it in to a depth of 5-10cm (2-4in). He starts sowing only when the ground temperature has stayed above 7°C (45°F) for at least a week.

Seed packets usually indicate sowing depths, but as a general rule most vegetable seed should be sown about 1.5cm (½in) deep; exceptions are beans (broad, French and runner), which should be sown about 4cm (1½in) deep; peas and sweet corn about 3cm (1¼in) deep; and courgettes, squashes, marrows and cucumbers about 2cm (¾in) deep. On lighter, sandier soils, sow slightly deeper. When sowing outdoors Mike uses a string guide and a measuring stick to ensure the orderly straight lines befitting a Victorian kitchen garden.

BELOW The restored vinery is an ideal spot to cossett young plants prior to planting out. OPPOSITE The performance and flavour of most plants varies according to soil and climate.

WATERING

Generally, all seedlings and young plants need regular watering to encourage healthy root growth, but for more mature plants Mike recommends assessing their individual needs. For example, vegetables grown for their leaf tend to require a lot of water throughout growth, whereas fruiting vegetables (such as tomatoes, peas and beans) need watering most when plants have set flower and fruits begin to swell.

Use a fine mist or spray for seedlings and, once established, always water the base of plants rather than the leaves. Remember an occasional thorough soaking is far more beneficial than frequent sprinklings. To limit evaporation always water in the evenings

WEED CONTROL

Weeds compete with crops for light, moisture and nutrients and it is vital to keep the hoe moving during the growing season to keep on top of them. Knock back annual weeds as often as possible, and remember that they are at their weakest when they have just flowered but before they have set seed.

Perennial weeds pose more of a problem, as they are harder to control. The best method of eliminating them is to repeatedly cut them down and dig out all traces of root (do not add perennial weeds to the compost heap unless they have been completely dried out in the sunshine.). Alternatively, cut back top growth and cover the affected areas with thick black plastic sheets or carpet to eliminate all light. Leave for three months to a year, depending on the extent of the problem, checking periodically to see if the weeds have died. If necessary, crops can be grown through slits in the covering.

ENCOURAGING WILDLIFE

'There are lots of useful friends in the garden and we try to encourage them as much as possible,' says Mike. 'The most important thing is to offer wildlife a sanctuary, somewhere they can shelter from the worst of the winter weather, make nests and feel safe.' The kitchen garden's 2.7m- (9ft-) high brick walls, trained fruit trees and shrubs provide plenty of niches for birds and insects to set up home. Seed- and berry-bearing plants provide food for birds, and nectar-rich flowers, such as foxgloves, salvias and cosmos, attract beneficial insects. Ladybirds and lacewings are important predators of aphids, and mason bees are excellent pollinators, coming into the garden early in the year. 'Bees like flowers that they can crawl into best, whereas butterflies prefer more open, daisy-like blooms,' says Mike.

PESTS AND DISEASES

Mike's organic approach to pests and diseases in the kitchen garden is detailed below.

ASPARAGUS

ASPARAGUS BEETLE Attacks start in May/June when small black eggs are laid on the foliage. Larvae and adults feed on the foliage and, in extreme cases, will defoliate the plant. Spray with insecticidal soap to control. They can also be hand-picked and destroyed.

BEANS

BLACK BEAN APHIDS (BLACKFLY) These are a real problem for broad beans, dwarf French beans and runner beans. They will form clusters all over the stems, leaves and tips of the plants. If natural predators are unable to cope, then spray with insecticidal soap until the natural balance has returned. Sometimes pinching out the tips of plants as they come into flower will check the pest allowing the pods to swell.

ROOT ROT This can be controlled by crop rotation – simply growing on a fresh site each season.

BEETROOT

These are fairly trouble-free. Take care to not to damage the swollen roots as you hoe along the rows. Water regularly – this will prevent them becoming woody and unusable.

SCAB Affected roots appear to have a sunken scabby patches and/or scabby raised areas. Although these look unpleasant, the roots are perfectly usable. This disease is usually worse on light soils.

BRASSICAS

BIRDS Erect some form of net caging until the plants become established. If all else fails, Mike suggests eliminating the attackers with a well-aimed shotgun.

CABBAGE APHID Spray with insecticidal soap as soon as they are seen. Once they are able get under the heart leaves they are impossible to control.

CABBAGE ROOT FLY Cabbage root flies attack cabbages and cauliflowers soon after planting. The flies lay eggs just below the surface of the soil, quite close to the plant, then the hatched maggots feed on the roots and burrow their way through into the stems to pupate. Use square 15cm (6in) 'collars' made from damp-proof-

kitchen garden basics

course material at soil level to prevent an attack. The eggs are laid at the edge of the collar and the maggots perish before they can attack the roots and stem of the plant. If any plants are attacked, dig the entire plant out and burn it. Check carefully to make sure no maggots remain in the soil.

CABBAGE WHITE BUTTERFLY The caterpillars of both the large and small white butterflies and moth all feed on the leaves of brassicas, in extreme cases reducing them to lace curtains. It is the late summer broods that cause all the problems. To deal with small infestations, crush the eggs by hand and pick off the caterpillars. Larger colonies can be controlled by using *bacillus thuringiensis* (BT). It comes in powder form and is mixed with water to spray on to the leaves.

CLUB ROOT This is a problem on cold, wet, acidic soils. The pH needs to be at least 6.5 to be safe, so carry out a soil check to confirm what remedial action needs to be taken to alter the pH. Usually all that is required is a dressing of ground chalk, lime, or calcified seaweed to raise the alkilinity.

FLEA BEETLE These will attack the seed leaves of all members of the brassica family. It is only serious in dry weather and can be controlled by watering the foliage during the cool of the evening. Once the true leaves begin to grow, the problem will cease.

BRUSSELS SPROUTS
See brassicas.

CABBAGE
See brassicas.

CARROTS
CARROT ROOT FLY This pest can completely destroy a crop. The fly is at its most active during May and June so by varying sowing dates much of their potential to cause damage can be avoided. Make the earliest sowings during March to provide a crop in June/August. Follow on by sowing the main crop during late June/July. In both cases, sow the seed as thinly as possible to avoid having to over-thin the seedlings afterwards. The scent of the freshly crushed foliage attracts the female fly, inviting her to lay her eggs in the soil near the crop. Thinning after rain or in the cool of the evening helps to fool her ladyship. It's also worth watering along the rows before thinning. Another tip is to keep drawing the soil up over the shoulders of the carrots, always leaving a tuft of foliage to grow on.

SPLITTING This is the result of erratic watering. If you soak the row well at least once a week during dry conditions in good soil full of organic material, it is not a major problem. Always select a variety to suit the soil: short stump rooted types for hard, stony ground; long tapering roots can only be produced in fibrous soils.

WIREWORM This can be a problem on recently broken ground. Try growing early, quick-maturing varieties and harvest when young. After the first season they should not be a problem.

CAULIFLOWER
See brassicas.

CELERIAC
See celery.

CELERY
LEAF MINER
See parsnips.
LEAF SPOT Brown patches appear on the leaves and stems of the plants. It is usually a seed-transported disease, so always buy clean, reliable seed.

CUCUMBERS, MARROWS, COURGETTES
CUCUMBER MOSAIC VIRUS Affected plants have puckered, distorted leaves that are yellow with dark green patches. Remove and destroy these plants before they infect others around them. The virus has many host plants, especially weeds, so keep the plot as weed free as possible. Aphids act as vectors so spray with insecticidal soap to control them.
POWDERY MILDEW This problem is usually caused through dry soil at the roots. Water regularly to prevent the plants from becoming stressed.

FLORENCE FENNEL
Generally trouble free. It can be prone to bolting under cold or dry conditions.

GARLIC
See onions.

GLOBE ARTICHOKES
PETAL BLIGHT FUNGUS This will cause the heads to rot. Avoid over-feeding the plants, thereby producing soft vulnerable tissue. Remove all spent foliage at the end of the season.

LEEKS
Generally leeks are free of serious pests and diseases.
MILDEW See onions.
RUST Bright orange elongated pustules of spores can be seen on the leaves. Remove and burn all infected leaves, and rotate the site each season. Rust is more of a problem for the exhibitor – the leeks are perfectly edible.

LETTUCES
APHIDS Spray with insecticidal soap to control heavy infestations of greenfly, otherwise wash the lettuce heads thoroughly before eating them.

LEFT To protect tender young seedlings, Mike and his team make simple yet effective home-made bird scarers from batons of wood, nails and cotton thread (see p. 39).
OPPOSITE Onions must be properly dried and ripened before being stored in a light, airy, frost-free spot.

kitchen garden basics

MILDEW Sometimes the plants are attacked at soil level and rot off. Avoid planting too deeply and make sure that the soil is well prepared before planting out.

ONIONS

MILDEW This appears as grey/purplish streaks or spots on the foliage of the plants and is usually worse in cold, wet seasons. It is more disfiguring than damaging.

NECK ROT This will destroy onions in store. Always ensure that bulbs are properly dried and ripened before storing. It can be caused by bending the tops over before the bulb is ready. Always wait for the foliage to collapse in its own time before lifting the onion.

ONION FLY Without doubt onion fly is the most serious pest and is more of a problem on dry soils. Most of the damage is done around May to June, so water the plants well during this period. Dig up the entire plant and destroy it by burning, and also inspect the root area to ensure that no larvae are surviving in the soil.

PARSNIPS

CELERY LEAF MINER Celery leaf miner attacks parsnips, as well as carrots, celery, celeriac and parsley,

by tunnelling between the layers of leaf tissue. Brown blisters appear on the leaves any time after May. Remove the affected leaves, crush and then destroy them. Following this action, give the plants a liquid feed to boost re-growth.

PEAS

APHIDS (GREENFLY) If natural predators cannot cope, then spray the plant with some insecticidal soap until the natural balance is restored.

FOOT ROT This can damage plants and early varieties are especially vulnerable. To prevent foot rot, try to avoid creating heavy, wet soil conditions and change site each growing season.

MILDEW This can be a problem with later-maturing varieties. It can be caused by a lack of water at the roots, so prepare moisture-retentive soil, but not water-logged. Also, remove the spent haulms of earlier sown varieties, which can act as host plants for mildew.

PEA MOTH This problem is usually avoided by growing varieties that do not flower during June and mid-August when the moth is particularly active. For continued production, grow mangetout varieties

THRIPS These are not a major worry. Once the plants begin to grow away the problem is over. The only real damage is a slight scalloping of the leaf edges.

POTATOES

BLIGHT Probably the biggest problem with potatoes, blight is always more severe during warm wet summers when humidity is high. The spores are transported by rain, which makes the foliage extremely vulnerable to attack. In recent seasons it has been seen earlier and earlier, sometimes arriving in July. As soon as the

LEFT Tender cabbage seedlings are particularly attractive to birds and must be protected once planted out.
OPPOSITE Lettuces can be sprayed with insecticidal soap to deter aphids, but must be washed well before being eaten.

telltale brown spots are seen on the leaves, completely remove and destroy all foliage. It is important to prevent the spores from contaminating the soil where they can quickly infest the developing potato tubers. Do not attempt to store blighted tubers and never save them for using as seed. Buy new certified stock each season to control the risk of introducing potato blight to the soil.

SCAB Scab is only a problem on alkaline soil. Digging in organic matter will go some way towards controlling it. The unpleasant appearance is only skin deep, and it has no effect on the quality of the crop. Scab-resistant varieties are becoming increasingly available.

SLUGS Slugs and snails are worse wherever soil conditions are wet and heavy. Growing early varieties and making sure to lift them before September will ensure you get good crops.

WIREWORM Usually wireworm is only found on freshly cultivated grassland or land that has been long neglected. Some control can nevertheless be gained by pushing sections of carrot into the soil to attract the wireworm. These can then be collected and disposed of, destroying the pest along with the carrot. Regular cultivation will quickly eliminate wireworm.

SHALLOTS

See onions.

SPINACH

MILDEW Mildew is the main problem of spinach, usually caused through dryness at the roots or over-crowding of the plants. Thin the plants to at least 30cm (1ft) apart, and make sure the rows are well watered.

SWEET CORN

FRIT FLY The larvae of these will burrow into the tips of growing plants. This stunts their growth and also leads to twisted or damaged leaves. Try spraying with insecticidal soap. Sow under glass during April to avoid attacks to seed sown in open ground during May.

TOMATOES – OUTDOORS

BLIGHT This is the same blight that attacks potatoes, so take care to avoid growing tomatoes on land where you have previously grown spuds. Grow the more modern resistant tomato cultivars to avoid having to use copper-based fungicides. In recent years a citrus-based product called Bio-sept has offered some control against blight.

TURNIPS

FLEA BEETLE Flea beetle is really only a problem during hot, dry spells. They are easily controlled by watering along the rows of seedling during the cool of the evening. Sometimes known as turnip fly, flea beetle will attack the seed leaves of turnips; it is not a pest once the rough true leaves are produced. Fred Streeter, a lovely old gardener, wrote in an article that he used to control flea beetle by dusting along the rows, covering the wet foliage with fine soil collected after preparing seed beds. He claimed 'they didn't like getting the grit between their teeth'.

WORDS OF WISDOM

'The most important element in gardening is time,' says Mike. 'Try to create a garden that will give you the most satisfaction for the hours and effort that you can allocate. Grow crops that will give you a good return and don't bother with difficult crops unless you have lots of experience or time as they will invariably be a disappointment. The greatest pleasure of vegetable gardening is taking your produce home and eating it. Don't overwhelm yourself; it's there to be enjoyed.'

salads

Salad leaves are easy to grow and by selecting
suitable varieties and sowing in succession
you can pretty much ensure a year-round supply.

OPPOSITE Lettuce grow best in a cool position with
reasonably fertile, moisture-retentive soil. After years of
experimenting, Mike has found that lettuces with a red tinge,
such as this oak-leaved lettuce are particularly sturdy.

salads

LETTUCE, ROCKET, CHICORY AND ENDIVE

There is a vast range of different salad leaves available, and their varied tastes, textures and shapes mixed together in a bowl are a delicious way of eating fresh, nutritious greens. Salad leaves are easy to grow, and by selecting suitable varieties and sowing in succession you

but they can be broadly divided into hearting (a tight, infolded head of growth) and non-hearting varieties.

Lettuces need reasonably fertile, moisture-retentive soil and plenty of water to make them juicy and sweet. 'They don't like excessive heat, so are best planted in a cool spot, but don't worry if they bolt, just keep planting and replace as required,' advises Mike. 'Some varieties are better than others at coping with the adversities of the British climate, but we find that those with a red tinge are the most resilient.'

Early varieties can be sown from mid-February onwards. Start them off indoors in trays or modules, sowing thinly, then plant out in mid-March, 15–23cm (6–9in) apart (appropriate to the final size). Warm the soil a fortnight or so before by covering with cloches or weighted-down plastic sheets. Continue sowing at 10–14 day intervals, and begin direct sowing outdoors from mid-March.

> 'LETTUCE DELIGHTETH TO GROW IN A MANNURED, FAT, MOIST, AND DUNGED GROUND; IT MUST BE SOWEN IN FAIRE WEATHER IN PLACES WHERE THERE IS PLENTY OF WATER AND PROSPERETH BEST IF IT BE SOWEN VERY THIN. IT MAY WELL BE SOWEN AT ANY TIME OF THE YEARE, BUT ESPECIALLY AT EVERY FIRST SPRING, AND SO SOONE AS WINTER IS DONE, TILL SUMMER BE WELL NIGH SPENT.' *GERARD'S HERBAL*, 1597

can pretty much ensure a year-round supply. Quick-maturing crops, such as lettuce and rocket, are ideal to grow alongside slower-growing vegetables as a simple way of optimizing space.

Before sowing salad crops it is worth raking over the soil to a fine tilth and removing any large stones, then it is simply a matter or weeding and watering during the growing season.

Hardy varieties sown in September will overwinter outside, but they will benefit from some form of protection, such as a cloche or fleece. During the winter months Mike grows lettuce in the glasshouse. 'We plant them in 10cm (4in) pots, but old grow bags freshened up with a slow-release fertilizer are ideal,' he says.

Cut-and-come-again varieties, which can usually be cropped twice, are a particularly good way of maximizing space. 'I wait until the first growth gets about 5–8cm (2–3in) high before trimming it off, then leave the second growth to form a good heart.'

Keep plants free of weeds and water regularly in dry weather. Slugs and snails are common pests, particularly with tight-leaved varieties that provide plenty of nooks and crannies in which to hide.

LETTUCE *Lactuca sativa*

Lettuce is an excellent source of phytochemicals as well as a source of vitamins A, B and C, calcium, potassium and fibre. Its soporific effect (caused by the milky latex found in the leaves and stems) has been acknowledged since early times, and it is believed the Romans used lettuce as a sleeping aid.

There are many different varieties of lettuce available, including butterhead, cos, loose leaf and crisphead,

THIS PAGE Before sowing salad crops, rake the soil to a fine tilth and remove any large stones.

ROCKET *Eruca vesicaria* subsp. *sativa*

This aptly named, fast-growing annual – also known as arugula, rucola or roquette – originates in southern Europe. Cultivated since Roman times, its distinctive tasting, spicy leaves are great for pepping up a mixed salad, and contains vitamin C and potassium. (Rocket flowers are also edible, packing the same punch as the leaves.) Dioscorides (40-90AD), the Greek physician and pharmacologist who wrote *De Materia Medica*, the definitive book on herbal medicine for around 1,600 years, described rocket as 'a digestive and good for ye belly'. There is also a wild form of rocket, a perennial, which is less productive with slightly coarser leaves, but has more drought tolerance.

Cultivated rocket is a fairly hardy crop that grows in most soils but does best in shade as it tends to run to seed quickly in extreme heat. Sow outdoors from March until end September in drills, or broadcast and thin to 15cm (6in) apart. 'Rocket has a short reproductive cycle so it's a constant battle to hold it back. Sow it weekly to ensure a good supply, and water regularly to keep leaf growth nice and plump,' says Mike. Harvest within three to four weeks by picking the outside leaves and allowing the younger growth to increase in size.

OPPOSITE Marvel of Four Seasons is one of Mike's favourite lettuces. ABOVE A young seedling. RIGHT Early varieties can be started off indoors in trays or modules from mid-February onwards and then planted out in mid-March.

salads

CHICORY (RADICCIO)
Cichorium intybus

Native to Europe, chicory is a hardy perennial grown as an annual. It has been cultivated for centuries and is particularly popular in Italy. Mike grows certain varieties for their distinctive, bitter-tasting leaves and others (known as witloof, or Belgian chicory) to force and blanch indoors in winter for their mild-flavoured, white leaf buds, called chicons. During the Napoleonic wars, when coffee supplies were cut off, the English made a coffee substitute from ground, roasted chicory root. It is still popular today as a caffeine-free drink.

With its strong constitution, chicory is fairly easy to grow and is very useful as a winter salad because it can be harvested late in the season. Leaf chicory is usually eaten raw, although some varieties can be cooked; chicons are particularly good braised. Chicory contains vitamin A, folic acid, calcium, iron and fibre.

Chicory should be thinly sown in wide drills from spring onwards, and thinned to 15–20cm (6–8in) apart. It does best on light, deeply dug, well-manured soil in an open site. 'It is as straightforward to grow as lettuce, but is tougher and less likely to bolt,' says Mike.

Radiccio, or red chicory, is relatively hardy and has stunning red leaves, the colour of which intensifies with cold weather. 'Sown in July it will overwinter and provides a good out-of-season supply as well as a much needed splash of colour to the garden,' says Mike.

OPPOSITE Mike grows witloof chicory for forcing indoors during winter for its tender white leaf buds, which can be eaten braised or raw. Dig up the tap roots in October and trim off the top growth. BELOW, LEFT TO RIGHT Cut the foliage to about 5cm (2 in) using a clean, sharp knife or a pair of secateurs.

Mike sows witloof varieties outdoors in May to get decent-sized roots for winter forcing. Sow thinly in drills and thin to 23cm (9in) apart once they have their first true leaves. Apart from weeding, they require little attention. 'If plants are left, they will run to seed but you can get an extra crop by suspending the growth and tricking it to grow again,' explains Mike. Dig up the chicory in October, check that the tap root is healthy and trim to about 15-20cm (6-8in), cutting off any side shoots. Use a clean, sharp knife, and leave about 5cm (2in) of top growth. To hold them back until you want to force them, pack horizontally 2-3cm (1in) apart into boxes filled with almost dry sand or old potting compost, and store in cool to cold conditions.

From December, Mike plants four or five roots in a 30cm (12in) pot with multipurpose compost or garden soil, leaving the crowns exposed, and inverts another pot on top, covering up the base hole to block out all light. 'You don't need to supply them with nutrients, just an anchor zone,' explains Mike. The pots are then brought into a warmer environment (14-15°C/57-59°F) and watered moderately. Alternatively, blanch chicory in situ by covering the trimmed leaves with a light-proof container. The chicons should be cut off at soil level when they reach 15-18cm (6-7in) high. 'It's a simple but effective technique and you end up with nice crunchy, bittersweet leaves that are good chopped up and eaten raw,' says Mike.

ENDIVE *Cichorium endivia*

This lettuce-like plant is related to chicory and also has a distinct, slightly bitter taste. Endive's exact origins are unknown, but it is believed to have been introduced into northern Europe in the 1500s. It contains significant

OPPOSITE Plant four or five witloof chicory roots in a 30cm (1ft) pot making sure the crowns are exposed. Cover with another pot and exclude all light. Bring into a warm environment and water moderately. Cut chicons when they are 15–18cm (6–7in) tall.

amounts of vitamin A and folic acid as well as calcium, iron and fibre. Endive is very hardy and can be grown during the winter season without heat. It is best grown in reasonably fertile soil and needs regular watering.

Mike begins sowing in late spring, planting 30-35cm (12-14in) apart, and repeat sows until September with the appropriate variety. There a two main sorts of endive: those with a tight-growing habit that are self-blanching and those with a looser habit that can be blanched in situ to make them sweeter by covering dry heads with a plate or saucer to cut out the light. With the help of an Italian volunteer at Audley End Mike has tried blanching different sorts, but so far with little success. 'It seems the leaves are prone to rot in the British climate. So far, we've had better results from self-blanching varieties such as Cornet de Bordeaux and Fine de Louvier,' says Mike. Endive can be harvested as a cut-and-come-again crop; although those that have been blanched tend to be weakened by the process and may not resprout.

RECOMMENDED VARIETIES
LETTUCE
Batavia: La Brilliante, Vision. **Butterhead:** Buttercrunch, Continuity, Marvel of Four Seasons. **Cos:** Little Gem, Remus, Ruben's Red. **Crisphead:** Roxette, Webb's Wonderful. **Cut and come again:** Bianca Riccia, Bionda a Foglia, Saladini. **Looseleaf:** Amorina, Frisby, Salad Bowl. **Winter:** Rouge d'Hiver, Valdor, Wendel, Winter Density.

ROCKET
Rocket Rucola.

CHICORY
Catalogna, Grumolo Verde, Rouge de Trevise, Sugar Loaf, Witloof/Belgian.

ENDIVE
Cornet de Bordeaux, Fine de Louvier, Stratego.

pods & seeds

Peas and beans are some of the easiest crops to grow and their sweet, juicy flavour is far superior to their shop-bought counterparts.

OPPOSITE Mike enjoys experimenting with unusual varieties, such as Ezethas Krombeck Blauwschok, which has violet flowers and pods that contain green peas.

pods & seeds

PODS AND SEEDS

RUNNER BEANS, FRENCH BEANS, BROAD BEANS,
PEAS, ASPARAGUS PEAS AND SWEET CORN

Peas and beans are some of the easiest vegetables to grow and the juicy flavour of freshly picked crops is how they should really taste. 'They bear no comparison to shop-bought produce,' says Mike. In addition, bacteria in their root nodules fix nitrogen from the air into the soil and consequently peas and beans are ideal crops to precede heavy feeders such as members of the brassica family. Mike plants according to his four-year rotation system to avoid soil-borne diseases.

RUNNER BEANS
Phaseolus coccineus

Originating in South America, runner beans are tender, vigorous, climbing perennials that are grown as annuals for their edible pods and seeds. Many reach heights of around 3m (10ft), and there are some dwarf varieties, too, although these tend to yield fewer beans). Runner beans are an excellent source of phytochemicals as well as a supply of vitamins A, B1, B8 and C, and calcium, iron and phosphorus.

Sown in spring, the long, flat pods are ready for harvest from mid-summer until the first frosts, and they are best cropped before the edge of the bean becomes stringy. At the end of the season they can be allowed to run to seed and the beans stored dried. 'Up until Queen Victoria's reign runner beans were grown purely for their flowers,' Mike says.

Runner beans prefer an open, sunny, sheltered position, with well-drained, moisture-retentive soil that has had plenty of organic matter incorporated. They are not frost tolerant and do best in hot temperatures. Mike sows under glass in April, with one bean per 10cm (4in) pot, to plant out in mid-May. He prepares the ground at the end of the previous summer by digging a 60cm (2ft) deep, 1m- (3ft-) wide trench and gradually filling it up with annual weeds and waste plant matter from around the garden, then closes it up in early March with the original soil. 'Runner beans root deeply so it is important to have a mass of moisture-retentive material beneath them,' says Mike. If you are unable to prepare the ground in this way, do not be discouraged, just open up a trench in early spring and fill with organic matter such

as well-rotted compost or manure; if this is unobtainable, use shredded, wet newspaper then refill with soil.

Before planting, erect a sturdy support structure of 2.5m- (8ft-) long hazel or bamboo poles directly above the trench. Insert poles 60cm (2ft) deep into the soil for stability, and space them 30cm (1ft) apart to form either a wigwam shape or an arched tunnel. Plant beans alongside the poles and, as they grow, remember to tie in loosely. Runner beans must be watered well once the flowers have set and the beans have started forming. Mike recommends flooding them once a week. Keep the area weed free, particularly while plants are establishing. In a good season, beans can be harvested from July until October and should be picked regularly.

Runner beans can have a problem setting flowers. This often occurs in a cold, wet season when pollinators are not so prolific. Mike has found that those with pink and white flowers tend to suffer less, and choosing a sheltered spot will encourage bees and other insects.

FRENCH BEANS (HARICOT, KIDNEY BEAN) *Phaseolus vulgaris*

Also native to South America, French beans are very productive, half-hardy annuals grown for their delicate tasting edible pods, which can be eaten whole when immature or shelled for the beans (flageolets) when semi-mature. 'French beans form the backbone of our bean supply,' says Mike. They come in climbing and dwarf varieties and are similar to runner beans in many ways, although they are more tolerant of lower temperatures. French beans are available in a wonderful array of colours, from flecked to purple, golds and greens, and the pods can be round, oval or flat in cross-section. They are rich in protein and contain folic acid, potassium and beta carotene.

For the earliest sowing, Mike uses the darker-seeded types as they are better at coping with cold, damp conditions. He sows dwarf varieties singly into pots under glass during April, and from May to July

ABOVE Young seedlings of Crimson Flowered broad beans.
OPPOSITE Runner beans are vigorous climbers, with some varieties such as Painted Lady reaching about 3-metres tall. Planted in spring, their long flat pods should be ready to harvest from mid-summer until the onset of the first frosts.

transplants them in open ground, 5cm (2in) deep, 15-18cm (6-7in) apart, in rows 45cm (18in) apart. He also directs sows in May and June. Climbing varieties are grown in the same way and planted out 30cm (1ft) apart in double rows 60cm (2ft) apart or trained up wigwams.

Harvest beans 60-70 days after sowing and pick regularly to encourage a good crop. Check they are ready by snapping them in half, when they no longer snap leave them to mature and use as dried beans (which must be cooked before eating).

BROAD BEANS *Vicia faba*

This cool-season, annual crop is believed to originate from the Mediterranean and has been cultivated since at least 6800BC. Broad beans are particularly hardy and many varieties can even survive frost. They are grown chiefly for the large mature beans, which are shelled and eaten either cooked or raw. Alternatively, pods can be picked when immature and eaten whole, either boiled or steamed. Broad beans have a high nutritional content and provide a valuable source of protein as well as fibre, potassium and vitamins E and C. 'They are a very straightforward plant and deserve a place in every kitchen garden,' says Mike, 'and, as a bonus, the flowers are beautifully scented.'

Although many varieties of broad beans are suitable for overwintering, Mike has given up on autumn sowings as he has found that the plants at Audley End suffered badly in cold, wet conditions. 'We get a better return by sowing under glass from mid-January onwards and transplanting them into the garden from early March when they are a 5cm (2in) or so high and the roots are beginning to show through the bottom of the pot,' he explains.

Broad beans like an open, sunny site that is fairly sheltered from strong winds. They do best in well-dug, moisture-retentive, free-draining soil that has been manured the previous winter. Mike direct sows from February to May, planting in double rows with 23cm (9in) or so between plants and 30cm (1ft) between rows. 'Obviously you have to make the best use of space, but wider spacings allow for better air circulation and make for healthier plants,' he says. There are many old sayings governing the planting of beans, and one of the best known is: 'One for rook, one for crow, one to rot, one to grow.'

Dwarf varieties need no support, but with taller varieties Mike advises putting a couple of sturdy canes at either end of the rows and running lengths of string between to hold plants upright.

Blackfly are a broad bean's main enemy. From late April the aphids form clusters around the tips, weakening the plant and reducing yields. Ladybirds will feed on the blackfly, but if the problem becomes severe, spray the plants with insecticidal soap. Many people pinch out the tips once the flowers have formed as a means of preventing infestations and diverting energy

RIGHT French beans can be eaten whole when immature or shelled for the beans (flageolets). OPPOSITE Before planting runner beans, erect sturdy supports for them to climb up. These wigwam shapes are made of hazel poles inserted 60 cm (2ft) into the ground and firmly held together at the top with twine. As the plants grow, tie them in loosely.

into the growing pods, but it is not strictly necessary. However, the young leafy tops can be steamed and eaten as a tasty spring green.

'Once pods have reached the size of your middle finger, they can be eaten whole,' says Mike. 'Otherwise, wait until the beans have matured a little and you can see them bulging through the pods.'

Always pick broad beans from the bottom of the plant upwards and harvest frequently. Generally, the crop is over by June to early July, and the area can then be cleared to make way for other crops. Cut plants off at soil level, remembering to dig in the roots to return nitrogen to the earth.

pods &
seeds

PEAS *Pisum sativum*

The origin of peas is uncertain, but these fairly hardy, climbing annuals have been cultivated in Europe since around 7000BC. 'The taste of freshly picked garden-grown peas is incomparable to those bought in shops, however, they are a bit of a luxury crop as they take up quite a bit of space for a relatively small return,' says Mike. Peas are a good source of phytochemicals and vitamin C, and a significant source of folic acid and vitamin B1. They also contain vitamin K, potassium and fibre.

Peas are divided into two varieties: shelling and mangetout. With shelling varieties only the seed is edible, but with mangetout types both pod and seed are eaten. Mangetout are further subdivided into two categories: flat podded, which are eaten as immature pods; and sugarsnaps, which have rounded pods tightly packed with sweet-flavoured peas.

Shelling peas are also labelled as earlies, second earlies and maincrop, according to the length of time from sowing to cropping. Earlies take about 70 days, second earlies 80 days, and maincrop 100 days. 'By selecting different varieties and successional sowing you can get peas for most of the season,' says Mike. If space is at a premium, he advises planting only main crop varieties as they grow tallest and give the highest yield.

Choose an open, sunny site with deeply cultivated, moisture-retentive, free-draining soil that preferably has had plenty of organic matter, such as compost and manure incorporated in the previous season; they do not do well in either drought or overly wet conditions. 'They appreciate a soil that's in good heart,' says Mike. Like beans, peas fix nitrogen from the air and thus do not need a nitrogen-rich soil.

Shelling peas come in round- and wrinkle-seeded varieties. 'Round-seeded varieties aren't as sweet-flavoured as the "wrinklies" due to their higher starch content, but have the advantage of being hardy so are best sown in the autumn for cropping in June,' explains Mike. He direct sows round-seeded peas in October for an early crop; wrinkle-seeded peas

(obvious by their shrivelled appearance) from March until the end of June at two-weekly intervals; and mangetout varieties from mid-March onwards. He also suggests sowing an early variety, such as Little Marvel, in late June to provide an autumn crop. 'You can start peas off under glass during February and transplant under cloches in March, but peas aren't happy grown in greenhouses and do much better out in the open.'

Prepare the soil by digging it over thoroughly, then take out two V-shaped drills, about 5cm (2in) deep and 15-23cm (6-9in) apart. Water thoroughly with dilute seaweed fertilizer, sow seeds 5cm (2in) apart, then gently draw the soil over the top. Mike also draws soil up to form small ridges on either side of the two drills to create a 'buffer zone' in order to protect delicate seedlings.

To prevent mice stealing newly sown peas – which they seem particularly fond of – Mike soaks seed in liquid seaweed fertilizer. Birds are also a major problem for pea-growers as they pluck seed out of the ground as well as attacking young plants. Mike and his team make simple bird scarers by positioning home-made, wooden T-bar shapes with nails hammered in the tops at either end of the rows and running black cotton thread between them. Alternatively, you can use galvanized chicken wire guards. The pea moth attacks during June and August, and Mike combats this problem by planting varieties that are ready to harvest before or after this troublesome period.

Once peas have reached 5-8cm (2-3in) in height and their tendrils start to reach out for support, put stakes in among the plants. 'We use lengths of brushy birch and hazel from a local wood, but you can also use galvanized chicken wire for them to climb up.' Just take

ABOVE Broad beans are incredibly easy to grow. They are a highly nutritious crop being a valuable source of protein, potassium and vitamins E and C. As a further bonus the flowers smell wonderful. The White Windsor and Green Windsor varieties are sown in spring. OPPOSITE The violet flowers of Ezethas Krombek Blauwschok.

into consideration how tall the plants will grow and make sure they are supported right up to the top – heights can range from 45-180cm (18in–6ft).

Apart from weeding, peas require little attention during the growing season. Mike only waters the plants once they have broken into flower, and he harvests early and regularly to encourage them to continue bearing pods.

ASPARAGUS PEAS (WINGED PEA) *Lotus tetragonolobus* (*syn. Tetragonolobus purpureus*)

The asparagus pea is in fact not a pea at all, but a rather odd-looking four-winged bean that grows on a low, sprawling bush. Native to southern Europe, this half-hardy annual prefers an open, sunny, but sheltered spot with rich, light, free-draining soil and should be rotated around the garden with members of the pea family. Asparagus pea contains a small amount of fibre, iron and carbohydrate. Direct sown 30cm (1ft) apart in late April, the crinkled pods should be ready for cropping from end of July. Pick when they are no more than 2.5cm (1in) long; any longer and they become woody and unpalatable. They are eaten whole, steamed or

pods & seeds

ABOVE Asparagus peas grow on low sprawling bushes and should be cropped when they are no more than 2.5cm (1 in) long. OPPOSITE Mike grows some peas in pots indoors, such as Prince Albert.

lightly boiled, and have a vaguely asparagus-like flavour, but the main reason Mike grows asparagus peas is for their beautiful, dark-red flowers.

SWEET CORN (INDIAN CORN, MAIZE, CORN ON THE COB)
Zea mays

Sweet corn is a half-hardy annual grown for its cobs of edible seeds. It thrives best in hot, sunny conditions and a fairly long growing season. Believed to have been first cultivated in Mexico, sweet corn was introduced into Europe in the 16th century and soon became a staple crop. The sweet, juicy seeds, known as kernels, contain

a significant source of vitamin B1 as well as potassium and fibre. Each plant normally produces a couple of cobs – four at the very most.

Easily grown from seed, sweet corn does best if direct sown outdoors in early summer as it is slow to germinate in soil temperatures below 13°C (55.5°F) and hates root disturbance. Mike uses cloches or fleece to warm the ground at least ten days prior to planting and chooses a sunny, sheltered position with light, moisture-retentive, free-draining, moderately fertile soil. 'Bear in mind that at full height the plants can reach up to 1.8m (6ft) tall and will cast substantial shade,' says Mike.

Being a member of the grass family, sweet corn is wind pollinated and therefore must be sown in blocks at least four rows wide. Germination can be erratic, so always use fresh seed and never sow on a wet day as sweet corn has a tendency to rot. Space taller varieties about 60cm (2ft) apart in either direction and shorter ones 45cm (18in) apart. Grow supersweet varieties at least 8m (26ft) away from others to prevent cross pollination. To improve drainage, Mike makes small craters 8-10cm (3-4in) in diameter into which he drops three seeds. Once germinated he carefully thins out the two weaker seedlings.

Protect young plants from birds and weed rows regularly. When the tassels begin to appear at the top, keep plants well watered and if necessary use stakes to support stems. Once the cobs have formed, wait for the silky tassels to turn black before harvesting – usually in mid-summer to late autumn.

To ensure that the cobs are sweet, succulent and at their very best, pick them when the sugar content is highest. Mike tests for this by opening up the protective outer sheath and digging his thumbnail into the kernels. If a white milky sap spurts out, harvest them by snapping the cob clean off the stem. For the maximum flavour, it is best to eat the cobs as soon as possible after picking. 'We have a pan of water on the boil as we pick them,' laughs Mike.

1 Mike starts off early varieties of peas under glass during February then tranplants under cloches in March. 2 Birds will happily pluck fresh seed out of the ground and attack the tender young growth of peas, so take care to protect. Mike uses home-made bird scarers made from batons of wood, nails and cotton thread. 3 Galvanised steel mesh (chicken wire) is a good way of protecting young growth. 4 When peas reach 5–8cm (2–3 in) in height stake them by inserting bushy branches of birch or hazel along the length of the row. 5 The peas' tendrils reach out for support and plants can range from 45–180cm (1ft 3in – 5ft) tall.

pods & seeds

RECOMMENDED VARIETIES
RUNNER BEANS

Czar: white-seeded variety, which can be used as butter beans. **Desirée:** stringless, high-yielding and tasty. **Red Flame:** early variety; suitable for later sowing in colder areas. **Scarlet Emperor:** the yardstick by which all other runner beans are judged; pick young and tender. 'Cooked and served with butter and pepper, they are a meal fit for a gardener,' says Mike. **White Emergo:** white-flowered variety.

DWARF FRENCH BEANS

Aiguillon: resistant to bean mosaic and anthracnose. **Canadian Wonder:** bean seed good dried and used for cooking. **Hildora:** yellow bean that grows well during hot weather and is tolerant of bean mosaic. **Purple Queen:** purple pods that turn green when cooked.

CLIMBING FRENCH BEANS

Barlotta Lingua di Fuoco: red-striped pods and coloured beans. **Blauhilde:** strong grower with purple pods. **Eva:** dark green oval pods; resistant to mosaic virus; suitable for greenhouse or polytunnel. **Neckar Queen:** stringless oval pods; tolerant of the vagaries of the British climate.

BROAD BEANS
AUTUMN/SPRING SOWING

Aquadulce Claudia or Super Aquadulce: long pods; reliable and productive. **Futura:** tolerant of chocolate spot. **The Sutton:** excellent dwarf variety (30cm/1ft high), suitable for small gardens.

SPRING SOWING

Bunyards Exhibition: Victorian variety produces good crop. **Stereo:** Produces small white beans; young pods are suitable for eating as mangetout. **Green or White Windsor** varieties.

PEAS
Round seeded

Douce Provence: traditional French variety; tender and sweet. **Meteor:** low-growing; good for small gardens. **Pilot:** tall; crops well; probably the hardiest variety.

Wrinkled
EARLY VARIETIES

Early Onward: classic variety; ready in about 80 days. **Little Marvel:** early dwarf variety; sweet and juicy.

MAINCROP VARIETIES

Cavalier: long double pods with up to ten peas; resistant to powdery mildew. **Greenshaft:** early maincrop; resistant to mildew and fusarium wilt. **Onward:** heavy cropper; ready in 90 days. **Rondo:** double-podded; resistant to fusarium wilt.

MANGETOUT

Carouby de Mausanne: tall with purple flowers. **Ezethas Krombek Blauwschok:** violet flowers and pods containing green peas. **Norli:** true French mangetout; resistant to fusarium wilt. **Oregon Sugar Pod:** fast-growing, tall cultivar; best picked just as peas are forming.

SUGARSNAP TYPES

Sugar Ann: tall; ready in 90 days; resistant to fusarium wilt. **Sugar Rae:** dwarf variety.

ASPARAGUS PEAS

No named varieties.

SWEET CORN

Double Standard: good flavour; yellow and white kernels; ready in 80–90 days. **Kelvedon Glory:** reliable; early, heavy cropper; fine flavour. **Sweet Nugget:** supersweet variety; main crop ready in September; large cobs; grows well in cool conditions.

root crops

Root crops grow best in soil with a fine
even texture that has been deeply dug.
Keep them free of stones and lumps to ensure
plants can penetrate the soil effortlessly.

OPPOSITE Beetroot is grown for its swollen root, however,
its tender young raw leaves make an excellent addition to
salad; alternatively they can be cooked and eaten as spinach.

ROOT CROPS

BEETROOT, CARROTS, CELERIAC,
KOHLRABI, PARSNIP, RADISH, SALSIFY,
SCORZONERA, SKIRRET AND TURNIPS

Deep digging is the key to growing good quality long-rooted crops as it enables them to penetrate the soil effortlessly. Make sure that the soil is free of stones and lumps, and that it has a fine, even texture. Generally, root crops grow best in sandy loam and it is worthwhile doing what you can to make your soil imitate these qualities; heavy soils in particular will benefit from the addition of horticultural sand. Dig in plenty of

> 'THE BEETE IS SOWNE IN GARDENS: IT LOVETH TO GROW IN A MOIST AND FERTILE GROUND... THE JUYCE CONVEIGHED UP INTO THE NOSTRILS DOTH GENTLY DRAW FORTH FLEGME, AND PURGETH THE HEAD... THE GREATER RED BEET OR ROMAN BEET, BOYLED AND EATEN WITH OYLE, VINEGRE AND PEPPER, IS A MOST EXCELLENT AND DELICAT SALLAD...' *GERARD'S HERBAL*, 1597

well-rotted organic matter during the autumn prior to planting, but do not plant on freshly manured soil as it has a tendency to make the roots fork.

BEETROOT *Beta vulgaris*

Mike grows beetroot for its swollen roots as well as its tender young leaves. The roots are usually boiled in their skins until tender, but they are also good roasted, or grated and eaten raw; the leaves can be added to salads or cooked in the same way as spinach. Beetroot contains a significant source of vitamin C and folic acid as well as potassium. Typically, beetroot have deep red flesh, but they can also be white, yellow or even red with concentric white rings. The shape also varies

and may be rounded or long and tapered. Believed to be native to Europe, beetroot is a biennial grown as an annual and does best in cooler weather as it has a tendency to bolt in heat.

Beetroot prefers a reasonably rich, free-draining, well-cultivated soil; do not plant in freshly manured ground as this can cause the roots to fork. Mike sows early, bolt-resistant varieties outside from the beginning of March onwards, in drills 1cm (½in) deep and 8-10cm (3-4in) apart. Alternatively, you can start them off under glass in modules in mid-February and plant out as young seedlings. 'With the older varieties one single seed is actually a cluster of seeds,' says Mike. 'We plant a three seeds (clusters) per station and expect to get nine beetroot back.' Continue sowing in succession, every two to three weeks, until mid-summer.

Protect young seedlings from birds with netting or bird scarers, then weed regularly during the growing season and water in hot dry weather, particularly in the early stages of growth. Harvest roots when they are a decent size – this is usually 6-12 weeks after sowing – after which time they become coarse and woody. Being fast growing, beetroots are ideal for catch cropping and intercropping.

CARROTS *Daucus carota*

Grown for their swollen roots, carrots are rich in beta carotene (vitamin A) and contain phytochemicals, vitamins C, D, E, K and B, and potassium. According to

OPPOSITE Mike sows early bolt-resistant varieties of beetroot in modules under glass in mid-February, then plants them out as young seedlings when the weather conditions permit. He harvests roots 6–12 weeks after sowing.

root crops

folklore, eating carrots helps you to see in the dark but this has not been proven scientifically.

Carrots are biennial plants grown as annuals, and although orange-fleshed types are the most usual, white, yellow and purple varieties are also available. In addition to the roots, carrots produce a pretty feathery foliage, which makes them popular in potagers. Native to Europe, carrots have been cultivated for centuries, although early varieties, such as those grown by the Romans, were branched.

Carrots do best in an open but sheltered position, with a reasonably rich, light, free-draining (preferably sandy) soil that has been deeply cultivated. Long-rooted varieties require a loose, deep soil to thrive, whereas those with shorter roots are suitable for shallow and heavy soils. Carrots can be grown in deep containers, such as an old chimney pot, filled with a loam-based compost. With the careful selection of varieties and successional sowing it is possible to crop carrots for about nine months of the year.

Carrots can be roughly divided into early and maincrop varieties. Mike favours the earlies and he harvests them when they are small and sweet and roughly the size of a finger, which usually takes about 10-12 weeks; maincrop carrots mature in 18-24 weeks and are generally larger. Start early, round varieties in modules under glass from late January onwards, making the last sowing no later than July. Carrot seed is particularly small, so take care to sow sparingly to reduce the need for thinning later on. After hardening off, early, round varieties can be transplanted outside, 5cm (2in) apart in rows spaced 10-15cm (4-6in) apart.

In late February to early March, Mike sets up cloches to warm the soil for a couple of weeks before the first direct sowing, which he either broadcasts or sows thinly in rows 15cm (6in) apart. He sows earlies in spring, making successional sowings up until July, and then at the beginning of August he sows early varieties again for a late crop.

In late June to early July, Mike sows the main crop in drills 15cm (6in) apart. 'By making a later sowing, we manage to miss out on the problem of carrot root fly, which is mainly active in May. Even with this later sowing we get a good harvest of decent-sized carrots,' explains Mike. The main crop will need thinning to allow for the larger sized roots, however, the thinnings can be eaten as a tender young crop. Maincrop carrots should be ready in late August to early September through to November.

During the growing season, keep beds free of weeds and mulch to retain moisture. The traditional method to discourage carrot root fly (which are low flying) is to erect a 50cm- (20in-) high barrier around the crop, or enclose with fine meshing. Carrot fly are attracted to the smell of the roots, so always carry out thinning and cropping on damp days to suppress the scent. Watering crops beforehand also helps. As plants get 8-10cm (3-4in) tall, draw up the soil to hide roots and confuse carrot fly. Some gardeners also swear that carrot fly can be discouraged by growing carrots near onions and garlic.

Harvest earlies by hand as soon as they are large enough to eat; lift maincrop varieties by easing them out of the ground with a fork while tugging at the tops. Carrots are moderately hardy and in favourable conditions can be left in the ground and lifted as required. Store in sand in cool, dry conditions or make a clamp (see p. 151).

CELERIAC *Apium graveolens* var. *rapaceum*

Celeriac is cultivated for its thick, bulbous root that has a strong taste similar to celery (to which it is related). It is also known as turnip-rooted celery. The roots are rich in potassium and can be grated for use in salads, or sliced and cooked in soups and stews.

A hardy biennial, celeriac is invariably grown as an annual and, although easy to cultivate, it needs a long

ABOVE Sow celeriac in March, prick out the seedlings into individual pots in April, then plant them outdoors at the end of May. Germination can take considerable time, but it is worthwhile being patient.

growing season in order to reach maturity. It has been cultivated in Europe for many years and was introduced into Britain in the early 18th century. Germination and the initial stages of growth can be slow, but it is certainly worthwhile being patient.

Mike sows celeriac in March either in modules, or in trays and then pricks out into pots in April. Harden off, then plant out at the end of May, 30-35cm (12-14in) apart in both directions. Celeriac does best in rich, fertile, very moisture-retentive soil in an open spot. 'They like bog-like conditions and you can't water them too much,' says Mike. Keep the soil free of weeds, and mulch to retain moisture.

Slugs are particularly partial to celeriac, so try to pick them off at night and encourage natural predators. 'Periodically peel the lower leaves off so that the plant resembles Bart Simpson,' says Mike. This exposes the crown and encourages the bulb to enlarge. Plants also benefit from a feed of dilute liquid fertilizer. Harvest as

required when roots reach about 13cm (5in) in diameter, any time from late September to mid-November. In some areas, celeriac will survive outside all winter long, but if you are in any doubt, it is best to lift them and store in sand or soil in a dry, frost-free place.

KOHLRABI
Brassica oleracea

This fast-growing biennial is grown as an annual for its swollen, fleshy almost spherical bulb that can be grated and eaten raw or cooked. Kohlrabi can be boiled, mashed and served with butter, made into fritters or added to soups and stews. It has a delicate, slightly nutty flavour similar to a turnip and is an excellent source of vitamin C. Kohlrabi is a member of the cabbage family, however, it copes better with drought and high temperatures than other brassicas and is less susceptible to pests and diseases. Taking just six to eight weeks to mature, kohlrabi is best sown little and often – making it ideal for catch cropping and intercropping. Mike often plants it between rows of Brussels sprouts as it requires the same conditions as other brassicas (relatively rich, moisture-retentive, free-draining firm soil in an open but fairly sheltered position).

Sow kohlrabi thinly, in situ, from April onwards until the end of July, in drills 1cm (½in) deep and 30cm (1ft) apart. Thin to 10cm (4in) apart when seedlings reach 2.5cm (1in) high. As a rough guide, use white/green varieties for early sowings and purple-skinned varieties, which are hardier, later in the season. Protect with cloches if necessary, water regularly and keep the area free of weeds. 'They are best harvested once they reach the size of a golf ball but are no bigger than a billiard ball,' suggests Mike.

PARSNIPS *Pastinaca sativa*

The parsnip is an important winter crop as it is extremely hardy and also an excellent source of vitamin C, folic acid, potassium and fibre. It is a biennial grown as an annual for its plump, tasty root, which tastes particularly good roasted.

Parsnips can take three to four weeks to germinate and require a fairly long growing season. Mike always sows fresh seed, planting it directly in the soil in mid-March through to mid-May.

Parsnips prefer an open, sunny or lightly shaded spot with free-draining, deeply cultivated, light, loose soil that has had plenty of organic matter incorporated. They also appreciate warm soil, so cover with cloches or fleece prior to sowing. Take out a drill and water with liquid seaweed before putting in two to three seeds per station, 23cm (9in) apart. Once germinated and the first rough leaves appear, thin to one per station (this procedure is best carried out in the cool of the evening to deter carrot fly). Parsnips dislike disturbance, so while thinning them out put two fingers either side of the strongest seedling and snap or snip off the other two, then settle the row by watering immediately afterwards. Mike often interplants parsnips with radish or lettuce to make good use of space and help delineate the row during germination.

During the growing season, keep the rows watered and free from weeds. 'Take care not to damage the shoulders of the young parsnips,' says Mike. Harvest from the end of November onwards, preferably after a frost, which gives them a fuller, sweeter flavour. 'You can store them in the ground until February, but they are so good that we've always eaten them by then,' he adds. When harvesting, first loosen the soil with a fork to avoid damaging the tapered roots.

OPPOSITE Celeriac prefer bog-like conditions and do best in fertile, highly moisture-retentive soil. Make sure to water them well during the growing season.

RADISHES *Raphanus sativus*

'Although associated with summertime, this is a cool-season, short-day crop that lends itself to late winter and early spring sowings. If grown during the hotter summer months they have a tendency to run to seed, so should be planted in a cool, shady spot,' says Mike.

Radish come in various shapes and sizes, and different varieties crop best in different seasons. Eaten raw, they have a hot, peppery flavour and crunchy texture, and provide a good source of vitamin C as well as a source of potassium and fibre. Believed to be native to Asia, radish have been cultivated for centuries. According to Herodotus (*c.*450BC), labourers building the Egyptian pyramids were given rations of 'radishes, onions and garlic', while in the 18th century, radishes were believed to aid digestion, relieve colds and help break down kidney stones.

Radish is a hardy, quick maturing crop that is remarkably easy to grow, and is ideal for intercropping. It does best in a light, free-draining, moisture-retentive soil that is reasonably fertile. Mike sows hardy varieties in January, 4–5cm (1½–2in) apart in drills 5mm (¼in) deep, or broadcast sows in shallow trenches of the same depth, thinning later. He then makes successive sowings every two to three weeks, always watering the drills with dilute seaweed fertilizer before planting, then raking dry soil over the top, gently patting it down to ensure good contact. Water frequently and harvest the crop after six to eight weeks as radishes are best eaten when they are young and tender.

SALSIFY *Tragopogon porrifolius*

Salsify, which is also known as vegetable oyster and oyster plant, is a hardy biennial grown as an annual for its small, tapered, creamy-white roots that are eaten boiled. It was recorded by the plant hunter John Tradescant the Young in 1656, so compared to many crops it is a relative newcomer. Similar to scorzonera (see p.52), salsify has a distinctive, delicate taste that is

root crops

reminiscent of oysters. It prefers an open, sunny position with free-draining, light soil. Always use fresh seed and sow from May, two to three seeds per station, 15–25cm (6–10in) apart and 2cm (¾in) deep, in drills at least 30cm (1ft) apart. Reduce seedlings to the strongest one in the cluster when they are 5cm (2in) tall, and keep the patch regularly watered and hand weeded. Harvest from early November, as required, taking care not to snap the roots. They can be left in the ground over winter, but it is wiser to lift and store in dry sand in a frost-free place. Salsify also has stunning purple flowers, which are edible. It is said to repel carrot fly.

SCORZONERA
Scorzonera hispanica

Scorzonera is a perennial that is grown as an annual for its long, black-skinned tapering root, the skin of which is scraped off to reveal a white flesh. It has a taste somewhere between that of a carrot and a parsnip, and it is grown in the same way as salsify (see p.51). Native to central and southern Europe, it has been cultivated in England since 1560. Peel scorzonera before boiling it in water that contains a little lemon – this stops them from discolouring. Like salsify, scorzonera is said to repel carrot fly.

SKIRRET *Sium Sisarum*

Skirret was a delicacy of 16th-century Europe until the arrival of the potato from the New World. It is a tough, perennial crop, which originated in the Far East, and is grown for its numerous, small swollen roots that look rather like dahlia roots.

Skirret has firm white flesh that is tender and slightly floury with a sweet taste similar to that of carrot, to which it is related (both plants belong to the Umbelliferae family). It can be grown from seed, offsets or root division. Sow seed in summer under glass and plant out 40cm (16in) apart when the seedlings have four or five leaves.

Skirret prefers a rich, moisture-retentive soil and should be watered thoroughly during the growing season. Plants can grow up to 1.7m (5½ft) tall. Divisions or offsets should be planted in March or April. 'Harvest from autumn onwards, taking bits of root the same size as your little finger,' says Mike. Cook and use in the same way as salsify and scorzonera.

TURNIPS *Brassica rapa*

'Turnips are a much-maligned vegetable,' says Mike. 'But they are simple to grow and they have a mild, nutty flavour that some liken to a chestnut. The trick is to grow them quickly, without checks and to harvest them while they are still quite small – no larger than a tennis ball.'

Turnips are a biennial member of the brassica family, cultivated as an annual for their swollen root and tender young leaves, which are delicious eaten as greens. They are an ancient food crop, cultivated since around 400BC and were known by Anglo-Saxons as 'naeps'. The roots can be eaten raw in salad or cooked – they are particularly good roasted, mashed or added to stews – and contain a significant source of vitamin C. The tops on the other hand are an excellent source of vitamin A, folic acid and calcium.

Turnips prefer a light, fertile, moisture-retentive, well-drained soil in an open, but sheltered site. Mike sows turnips successively from March up until early August and finishes harvesting them in October. Sow them in 1cm- (1½in-) deep drills, in rows 25–35cm (10–14in) apart, and thin to 15cm (6in) apart. It's also a good idea to plant them on ground that later crops, such as Brussels sprouts, will occupy. Keep them well watered and harvest after about six weeks.

OPPOSITE Tender young plants are vunerable to damage by birds. This simply devised bird scarer, made from a potato and pheasant feathers, casts a shadow similar to that of a bird of prey and frightens off smaller birds.

RECOMMENDED VARIETIES

BEETROOT
Barbabietola di Chioggia, Boltardy, Burpee's Golden, Libero.

CARROTS

EARLY
Amsterdam Forcing: suitable for the earliest sowings under glass or outdoors; cylindrical roots. Nantes 2: quick-growing; ideal for forcing; sow in February for harvesting in June; blunt roots. Parabel: ideal for sowing in modules; produces small round roots.

EARLY MAINCROP
Chantenay Red Cored: quick-growing variety, with short tapered roots; excellent texture and taste; delay sowing until the soil warms up. Fly Away: alleged to be carrot fly resistant; medium cylindrical roots. Kinbi: golden yellow carrot with short tapered roots. James Scarlet Intermediate: dual purpose; harvest the roots when young or allow them to grow on to lift during October; good for storing. Resistafly: good carrot fly resistance; suitable to use as baby carrots; long cylindrical roots. Stella: good on heavy soils; long cylindrical roots. St Valery: a proper carrot with long orangey roots; first-class flavour; excellent drought resistance.

LATE MAINCROP
Autumn King: reliable; good size, colour and flavour; excellent for storing; a gardener's carrot. Berlicum: needs good soil; produces long cylindrical roots of good colour and texture. Cubic: deep red colour; short tapered roots with good keeping qualities.

CELERIAC
Giant Prague, Tellus.

KOHLRABI
Azur star, Cindy, Trero.

PARSNIPS
Avonresister, Cobham Improved Marrow, Gladiator, Hollow Crown, Javelin, Tender and True.

RADISHES
Belrosa, Black Spanish Round, Cherry Belle, D'Avignon, Munchen Bier, Minowase, Neckarruhm Weis, Rondeel.

SALSIFY
Giant, Mammoth.

SCORZONERA
Habil, Russian Giant.

SKIRRET
No varieties.

TURNIPS
Atlantic, Golden Ball, Purple Top Milan, Snowball, Tokyo Cross, Veitch's Red Globe.

potatoes

Digging up your first ever home-grown pototes is said to be a life-changing experience, but eating them is even more of a thrill.

OPPOSITE Potatoes need very little attention during the growing season other than earthing up and keeping on top of the weeds. Mike follows his grandfather's advice of only watering potatoes once they have flowered, as this is when the tubers begin to set and swell.

potatoes

POTATOES *Solanum tuberosum*

Digging up your first ever home-grown potatoes is said to be a life-changing experience, but eating them is even more of a thrill. Potatoes are believed to have been cultivated as an edible crop in Peru more than 4,000 years ago. Discovered by the conquistadors in the 1530s, they arrived in Europe around 1570. Although slow to gain popularity, potatoes led to dramatic changes in European dietary habits and became one of the most important staple foods – providing an excellent source of vitamin C as well as significant amounts of B3, B6 and iodine.

BUYING

At Audley End, Mike grows only varieties that would have been grown in the Victorian period, but there's a wide range of cultivars to choose from – both heirloom and new. 'Performance and flavour vary according to soil and climate, so it's always a good idea to find out what grows well locally and then experiment to find your favourites,' says Mike. Although it is possible to propagate from seed, the best way to grow potatoes is from tubers, called, rather confusingly, seed potatoes. Always buy from a reputable source and ensure potatoes are certified disease and virus free. 'Avoid those with obvious signs of damage and give them a little squeeze to make sure they're nice and solid,' suggests Mike. 'Try and get them all roughly the same size, ideally something that will sit nicely in the palm of your hand.' Seed potatoes are categorized as first earlies, second earlies and maincrop varieties (according to the length of time they take to mature). By growing a selection, you can pretty much ensure a supply of potatoes for the best part of the year. Mike advises buying tubers early in January or February.

CHITTING

To gain a few weeks' precious growth while the weather conditions are still unsuitable, potato tubers can be sprouted indoors – a process known as chitting. There is some debate over the effectiveness of chitting; research shows that, although chitting can speed up development, it may decrease the overall yield and is not strictly necessary, particularly for maincrop varieties. However, if you do decide to chit tubers, start them off as soon as you've bought them. Don't worry about timing as potatoes have an inbuilt dormancy, which means that they won't break until the conditions are right. Lay the tubers in seed trays lined with newspaper, with the 'rose end' (the one showing the most buds) facing upwards. Keep in a cool, frost-free place with good light conditions but out of direct sunlight. Ideally, the sprouts should be short,

> 'THIS PLANT (WHICH IS CALLED OF SOME SKYRRETS OF PERU) IS GENERALLY OF US CALLED POTATUS OR POTATO'S... THEY ARE USED TO BE EATEN ROSTED IN THE ASHES. SOME WHEN THEY BE SO ROSTED INFUSE AND SOP THEM IN WINE: AND OTHERS TO GIVE THEM THE GREATER GRACE IN EATING, DO BOILE THEM WITH PRUNES AND SO EAT THEM: LIKEWISE OTHERS DRESSE THEM (BEING FIRST ROSTED) WITH OILE, VINEGER, AND SALT, EVERY MAN ACCORDING TO HIS OWNE TASTE AND LIKING. NOTWITHSTANDING HOWSOEVER THEY BE DRESSED, THEY COMFORT, NOURISH, AND STRENGTHEN THE BODY.' GERARD'S HERBAL, 1597

THIS PAGE Potatoes grow best in an open site with reasonably fertile, well-drained, moisture-retentive soil that has been deeply cultivated. Dig trenches 20–30cm (8–12 in) deep, preferably with 1 m (3 ft) between each trench. Traditionally, Good Friday is reckoned to be the ideal day to plant potatoes.

green, sturdy and about 2.5cm (1in) long by planting time. 'If you are concerned about frost, keep a couple of sheets of newspaper or a length of hessian and cover the tubers on frosty nights,' advises Mike.

PLANTING

Although potatoes will grow in a range of conditions, they do best in an open site with reasonably fertile, well-drained, moisture-retentive soil that has been deeply cultivated. Potatoes can tolerate acid conditions but a pH of 5-6 is ideal. Mike advises choosing a spot sheltered from the damaging effects of winds, particularly for the first plantings. 'Potatoes like to be comfortable in the soil, so it's a good idea to loosen it up by digging during the winter months and incorporating plenty of organic matter, such as well-rotted manure or compost.' Being prone to soil-borne diseases, such as scab and eelworm, potatoes should be rotated around the garden.

'To extend the season, Victorians would begin planting early varieties of potato in February, using rows of cloches to protect the plants from frost. But unless you've got lots of time, labour and money to spare, it's best to wait until March before planting,' says Mike. 'Hold off until the soil is above 5°C (41°F) at a depth of 10cm (4in) for three consecutive days before planting.' Traditionally, Good Friday is reckoned to be a good spud-planting day.

There are a number of different ways to plant potatoes, but at Audley End Mike digs trenches roughly the depth of a spade (20-30cm/8-12in), with a metre (about a yard) between each trench. 'Obviously you can have trenches closer together and many books recommend spacings of 50-75cm (20-30in) apart, but if

OPPOSITE Victorian gardeners were keen to extend the potato growing season and often grew them in large terracotta pots under protection. Tubers potted in August onwards will yield a crop of 'new' potatoes in time for Christmas.

you have the luxury of space, wider spacing allows for better air circulation and makes it easier to work between rows.' Ideally, trenches should be orientated north to south so that the sun will fall evenly on the rows. Once the trench is dug, put in a few centimetres (inches) of well-rotted organic matter or a dribble of pelleted chicken manure.

Mike plants tubers in sequence to spread the cropping season: earlies first, then second earlies a fortnight or so later, and maincrop varieties a fortnight after that. 'When planting earlies try and anticipate when the last frost will be. Ideally, plants should be either under the ground or have a reasonable amount of growth on them in order to be able to cope. But don't panic if they do get frosted. Just water the frost off the tops before the sun gets on them; it only sets them back a bit,' Mike advises.

Mike places the tubers, eye end uppermost, against one wall of the trench to keep them upright and then carefully pushes the soil over them to a depth of about 5cm (2in). 'If they do get knocked over, they'll still make it to the surface eventually, it just takes them that much longer – possibly up to a week,' he explains. Earlies are planted 38-45cm (15-18in) apart, and second earlies and maincrop 50-60cm (20-24in) apart.

EARTHING UP

When the plants have grown 8-10cm (3-4in), draw the soil from between the rows up over the leaves to form a ridge – a process known as earthing up. 'We nurse the soil up like this a couple more times to increase the yield grown off the stem,' says Mike. 'It also stops tubers pushed up near the surface from becoming green and poisonous.' Mike gives the plants little more attention during the growing season, apart from weeding between rows and watering when necessary. 'My grandfather always used to say that the only time you need to water potatoes is after they've flowered, which is when the tubers begin to set and swell.'

potatoes

HARVEST

After the plants have flowered, check if the potatoes are ready by scraping away a little soil and feeling for decent-sized tubers. Earlies and second earlies generally take 12-14 weeks from planting to harvest and are best lifted as required. Maincrop take about 16-20 weeks and can be used fresh or stored. Mike advises lifting with a potato fork, which has flat, widely spaced tines. 'A potato fork has a happy knack of somehow being able to bend around potatoes rather than puncture them,' he says. Choose a dry, sunny day and lift the potatoes by forking around the plant to loosen the soil, then carefully shaking the tubers on to the earth's surface. Unless the potatoes are to be used immediately, leave them in the sunshine for 3-4 hours; that way the skins harden up and they keep better. Remove and destroy any that are damaged or diseased and transfer the rest to sacks made of hessian or thick brown paper, which should be secured at the top.

Store in a dark, frost-free place at around 4-10°C (40-50°F). Maincrop should keep until the following spring. Victorians would often store root crops over the winter months by building a clamp outdoors, and this method is still an excellent way of keeping many root crops (see Projects for instructions).

PESTS AND DISEASES

Potato growers are at the mercy of a whole host of pests and diseases. Mike's approach is one of prevention rather than cure. 'Give yourself a good start by buying clean stock,' says Mike, 'and always rotate crops in order to minimize soil-borne diseases.'

One of the most common and destructive diseases is blight, which starts as small brownish black spots or blotches on the leaves and stems and tends to strike in warm, humid conditions from mid-August onwards. One way to avoid its ravages is to grow only first and second earlies, both of which are harvested before blight can take a hold. If a plant does become affected, intercept the spores before they reach the tubers by removing and destroying all greenery. Water the plants, and they should continue to grow. Mike prevents scab (essentially a cosmetic disease caused by fungus that blemishes the potatoes' skin) by incorporating plenty of well-rotted organic matter into his trenches and thus reducing direct contact between the tubers and the soil. He also sprays plants with insecticidal soap to help combat aphids, which can transmit viruses.

GROWING IN POTS

It's possible to have a supply of home-grown potatoes for about nine months of the year, but there's often a bit of a gap between March and April. A good way to extend the potato growing season, and a method the Victorians were fond of, is to grow them in pots. Tubers potted from August onwards will yield a crop of 'new' potatoes around Christmas time, which somehow seems like a particular treat. Keep back a few healthy seed potatoes bought for early sowings and store in a cool, shady spot during the summer. Any variety will do, but Mike recommends earlies as they have compact growth and are quick to mature. However, he has also had great success with International Kidney, a maincrop variety.

Line the base of a 30cm (12in) pot with some multipurpose potting compost to a depth of about 7cm (2¾in). Plant no more than three sprouted tubers per pot, then half-fill with more compost. Keep in a frost-free place in direct sunlight. Water regularly and as the growth pushes through, top up with more compost to replicate the earthing up process discussed above. After flowering, poke around to see if the tubers are ready – roughly the size of a hen's egg – and harvest by gently tipping over and emptying the pot.

NOTE: The Henry Doubleday Research Association (HDRA) holds an annual Potato Day at Ryton Organic Gardens, near Coventry, where you can buy a huge range of organic potatoes. For information, call ++ 44 (0) 24 76 303517 or visit www.hdra.org.uk.

1

2

1 To grow potatoes in pots, line a 30cm (1ft) pot with multipurpose compost, plant no more than three sprouted tubers per pot and half fill with compost. 2 As plants grow, 'earth up' with more compost to increase the yield grown off the stem. 3 Keep pots in a frost-free place in direct sunlight. 4 Harvesting is easy, simply tip up the pot and poke around to find the potatoes.

3

4

potatoes

I A reel of string makes it much easier to dig a straight trench. 2 Ideally, trenches should be approximately a metre (yard) apart. 3 The best way to grow potatoes is from tubers called – rather confusingly - seed potatoes. 4 Ideally they should have a north-south orientation to ensure the sun falls evenly on the plants. 5 Place tubers eye end uppermost, against one wall of the trench to keep them upright. 6 Carefully push the soil over them to a depth of 5cm (2in). 7 During the growing season plants need little attention other than earthing up, weeding and watering as necessary. 8 After plants have flowered, you can check if the potatoes are ready by scraping away a little soil and feeling for decent-sized tubers. Harvest on a dry sunny day by forking around the plant to loosen the soil. 9 Carefully shake potatoes on to the soil's surface and leave in the sun for 3–4 hours; that way the skins harden up and they keep better. IO Check potatoes over and remove any that are damaged or diseased before storing in hessian or thick brown paper bags. RIGHT A potato fork, with its flat, widely spaced times, has a happy knack of somehow being able to bend around potatoes rather than puncture them.

RECOMMENDED VARIETIES
POTATOES
FIRST EARLIES
Accent, Epicure, Lady Christl, Sharpe's Express ('You won't beat them!'), Swift.

SECOND EARLIES
Arran Victory (purple skinned), Belle de Fontenay ('An exceptional salad potato'), Edzell Blue (purple skinned), Charlotte, Kestrel, Nadine, Nicola.

MAINCROP
International Kidney, King Edward (blotched, high-quality tubers), Majestic, Maris Piper, Ratte, Record.

IO

onion family

Members of the allium family – including garlic, leeks,
onions and shallots – are surprisingly easy to grow
and reputedly have many health-giving properties.

OPPOSITE Onions and shallots store well, but need to be
thoroughly dried before storing. After harvesting leave them
outside in full sunshine on wire netting, then hang them up
in a light, airy, frost free place.

onion family

GARLIC, LEEKS, ONIONS, SHALLOTS

Mike grows various members of the allium family, such as garlic, leeks, onions and shallots. 'They are easy to grow,' says Mike. 'Just make sure that you rotate these crops around the garden to avoid soil-borne diseases to which they are prone.' Members of the onion family grow best in an open, sunny spot in reasonably fertile, moisture-retentive, free-draining soil. They prefer a medium to light soil with a light, crumbly texture and must not be sown on freshly manured ground, or ground that has stagnant moisture.

GARLIC *Allium sativum*

Garlic is universally prized for its nutritional and curative properties. It is anti-viral, antibacterial and anti-fungal, and is a good source of phytochemicals as well as calcium, iron and vitamins A and C. The bulb, which forms underground over a long growing season, has a strong, distinctive flavour, and the young green stems can also be eaten fresh or cooked. Thought to originate from western Asia, this hardy perennial grown as an annual has been cultivated since Egyptian times. Garlic was not widely grown in Britain during the first part of the 19th century and this is attributed to anti-French feelings. But gradually people became accustomed to cooking with it and began to acknowledge its worth.

Bulbs are subdivided into thin-skinned segments, known as cloves, and their strength of flavour ranges from strong to mild, depending on the variety and growing conditions. Colour also varies from pink, white and purple. Mature bulbs can be used fresh or stored; some varieties have better keeping qualities than others.

When buying garlic for planting, Mike chooses good-sized bulbs with a firm texture and crisp

1 Harvest garlic when its leaves begin to turn yellow. 2 Loosen the soil with a fork and gently lift the bulbs out taking care not to damage the skin. 3 Bulbs are subdivided into thin-skinned segments known as cloves, which can be eaten fresh or stored. OPPOSITE Mike recommends spacing garlic at least 23cm (9in) apart in either direction. During the growing season he keeps the area free from weeds, but he doesn't water unless there are exceptionally dry conditions.

onion family

outer skin. 'Ideally, plump cloves should spill out when you crack the bulb open,' says Mike. Always buy fresh stock that is certified disease free and discard any weak or dried-out-looking cloves.

Garlic is divided into two categories: early planting and late. Most varieties appreciate a cool period, with temperatures below freezing actually proving to be beneficial. Plant early growing varieties

> 'THE LEEK BREEDETH WIND, AND EVIL JUICE, AND MAKETH HEAVY DREAMS; IT STIRRETH A MAN TO MAKE WATER, AND IS GOOD FOR THE BELLY: BUT IF YOU WILL BOIL A LEEK IN TWO WATERS AND AFTERWARDS STEEP IT IN COLD WATER, IT WILL BE LESS WINDY THAN IT WAS BEFORE. THE USE OF LEEKS IS GOOD FOR THEM THAT WOULD HAVE CHILDER.'
> WILLIAM TURNER, *HERBAL*, 1568

from mid-November up until the end of January, and later varieties any time during March. 'Garlic planted before Christmas seems to give better-quality bulbs with a superior flavour,' says Mike. 'And as the gardens begins to empty in autumn, it's a nice easy job to get out of the way.'

Mike uses a reel of string to line up the rows and, having the luxury of space, plants individual cloves 30cm (1ft) apart, in rows 30cm (1ft) apart. For those with smaller plots he recommends spacings of no less than 23cm (9in) apart. With the tip of a trowel or dibber he makes a small hole into which he places a single clove, flat end downwards, making sure that it sits just below the surface, then pushes soil back over the top. Hand weed to keep the area clean. 'Don't water unless exceptionally dry, as this decreases the intensity of their flavour,' advises Mike.

Harvest when the leaves begin to turn yellow, which, depending on the nature of the season, is usually by the end of June through to July. Loosen the soil with a fork, and gently lift out the bulbs, taking care not to damage the outer skin. Dry thoroughly then trim back the roots, before hanging up to store in a cool, frost-free, well-ventilated spot, ideally at about 5°C (41°F).

LEEKS *Allium porrum*

A hardy winter vegetable grown for their long, blanched leaf base, leeks have a delicate, onion-like flavour and are particularly good in soups. They have been grown since Egyptian times as a food stuff, and contain beta carotene, iron, potassium and vitamin C. Leeks are classified as early, mid- or late varieties, according to when they mature: the earliest types are ready in autumn, mid-season varieties from early to mid-winter, and lates the following spring. For a continuous supply, make successional sowings.

Although leeks can be grown in situ starting from early to mid-spring, Mike believes that you get better results by making the first sowings under glass from mid-February into March. Sow the seed in trays of compost, pricking them out after about six weeks and space them 5cm (2in) apart in 10cm- (4in-) deep boxes with adequate drainage. Transplant them to open ground in May into June, when they are about 10–30cm (4–12in) long and pencil thick.

OPPOSITE Makes the first sowing of leeks under glass from mid-February into March. Sow in trays of seed compost and after six weeks prick out seedlings into 10cm- (4 in-) deep boxes, spacing them 3cm (2in) apart.

I Ensure the soil has been well dug and use a dibber to make a row of planting holes. 2 When the seedlings are long and pencil thin, transfer them to open ground. 3 Trim root system with a clean, sharp knife. 4 Water each hole individually with dilute seaweek fertiliser. 5 Drop the seedling into the hole, where it should bob around like a little bouy. OPPOSITE Victorians favoured big leeks, whereas today's preference is for baby leeks. Smaller leeks can be obtained by dropping three transplants into one hole.

onion family

Ensure the soil has been well dug and large stones removed to facilitate growth. Leeks are hungry crops so it is a good idea to dig in plenty of organic matter prior to planting. Mike makes a row of holes with a dibber 15cm (6in) deep and 30cm (12in) apart. 'If you give the dibber a little twist it helps hold the soil in place,' he suggests. He waters each hole individually with dilute seaweed fertilizer after dropping a transplant into it. If the transplant has an extensive root system, he trims it back to about 1cm (½in). 'Don't worry if the leek bobs around like a little buoy,' says Mike. 'That's to be expected. You want it to fill up the hole eventually, so don't firm in – just allow the soil to fall in naturally.'

Water regularly until the plants are established and during very dry spells. Keep beds weed free and as the plants increase in size draw the soil up around them to increase the length of blanch. Harvest any time from November to the end of February. 'Victorians preferred them big, but today's fashion is for baby leeks,' says Mike. Leek size is dictated by space available, so to get mini versions he advises putting three transplants into a single hole. Having a long growing season, leeks can be intercropped with lettuces for optimum use of space.

ONIONS *Allium cepa*

'The allium family is reputed to have health-giving properties. My grandmother would eat onions raw, and she lived until she was 96,' says Mike. Onions are half-hardy biennials grown as annuals and come in brown-, white-, yellow- and red-skinned varieties. As with garlic, the intensity of flavour depends on the cultivar as well as growing conditions. Thought to be native to central or western Asia, the cultivation and use of onions in cooking dates back to antiquity. They are used extensively in cooking throughout the world, and provide a significant source of vitamins A and C, calcium, iron, potassium and fibre. The word onion comes from the Latin *unio*, meaning large pearl. Specific cultivars include salad onions, also called spring onions, which are cropped at an immature state for the young green leaves and small bulb, and pickling onions, which are densely planted and harvested when bulbs are thumb sized.

Onions can be produced from either seeds or sets. Onions sets have the advantage of being less labour intensive, maturing quicker, coping better with poorer soil conditions and less prone to disease. However, they are more expensive, bolt more readily than seed and fewer cultivars are available. Mike uses both methods and, with a combination of autumn and spring sowing, aims to extend the season in which they are available.

Onions grow best in soil that has been thoroughly dug and firmed. They have low nitrogen requirements and should not be grown on freshly manured ground. Pickling varieties are more tolerant of poorer soils.

Mike advises sowing onion seed under glass as early as possible 'preferably between Christmas Day and the New Year'. Sow seed thinly in trays of seed compost, covering them lightly. Prick them out when the seedlings have just begun to straighten up, transferring them into individual 8cm (3in) pots filled with potting compost. Harden them off, then plant outdoors in mid- to late spring, spacing them 15-23cm (6-9in) apart in rows 30cm (12in) apart. 'Try and get as many leaves as possible on a plant by the longest day, as after that they stop producing leaf growth and the bulbs begin to swell,' says Mike. He sows onion seed outside in short rows when the soil begins to warm up from mid-March onwards, aiming to transplant them into open ground 30cm (12in) apart in both directions by the end of April at the latest.

Onion sets are planted in spring in the same way as garlic, as soon as the soil conditions allow. Plant them with a space of 20cm (8in) between each set in rows 30cm (12in) apart. 'Choose firm, healthy-looking sets

OPPOSITE Mike grows onion seed under glass as early in the season as possible – ideally between Christmas and New Year. Sow thinly in trays of seed compost and prick out into individual 8cm- (3in-) pots when the seedlings begin to straighten up.

onion family

1 2 3

I Planting out onion seedlings. 2 Use a line and reel to ensure straight rows. 3 Bedfordshire Champion onions. 4 Take care not to damage onion bulbs when hoeing weeds. 5 To keep onions for storage, wait until top growth falls over before harvesting. 6 Use a fork to gently break the root system and let bulbs dry out on the soil surface prior to harvesting them. 7 Harvested bulbs. OPPOSITE Harvest onions for immediate use when they are a suitable size.

4

5 6

7

onion family

that are about the size of a marble, and cut off any wispy bits to prevent birds from pulling them out,' says Mike. 'Don't push sets into the soil as you can damage them and set up infection.' Overwintering onions sets, also known as Japanese onions, should be planted in situ from August to September and will be ready to harvest in June and July.

Protect sets from birds, keep beds weed free and water in the early stages of development only. Onions can be harvested for immediate use when they are a suitable size, but to keep bulbs for storage wait until the tops fall over naturally before taking them out of the ground. 'Put your fork underneath each onion and lift up enough to rip the roots and stop it growing,' says Mike. Wait for a week before taking out of the soil, then leave to dry on wire netting with the root base facing the sun. Hang dried bulbs in a light, airy, frost-free spot. 'Use those that are damaged, misshapen or have thick necks first. Smaller bulbs will keep longest and also have the most intense flavour,' explains Mike.

RECOMMENDED VARIETIES
GARLIC
Cristo: popular variety; produces high yield with strong flavour. **Early Wight:** autumn planting; early cropping; will keep but best used fresh. **Elephant garlic:** technically a leek; produces enormous, mild-flavoured cloves. **Printanor:** suitable for later planting in March. **Thermidrome:** autumn planting; short keeping quality.

LEEKS
Monstrous Carentan: fat stems; harvest mid-winter (October–January). **Musselburgh:** reliable old favourite; harvest from December to late March.

ONIONS
Bedfordshire Champion: simply the best. **Giant Zittau:** good flavour; excellent keeping qualities. **Red Brunswick:** mild-flavoured; the finest red onion.

PICKLING ONIONS
Paris Silverskin: small white onions. **Purplette:** red skin with white flesh.

SHALLOTS
Delvad: good flavour and keeping qualities. **Jermor:** French type; excellent. **Pikant:** first-class variety. **Sante:** red variety; don't plant until mid-March to prevent bolting.

SHALLOTS *Allium cepa* Aggregatum Group
Although often allied to the onion, a shallot's manner of growth is more like that of garlic, as both form multiple, new bulbs that are attached at the base. Shallots are used in much the same way as onions, but have a milder, more delicate flavour, and are a good source of phytochemicals, calcium, iron and vitamins A and C. They are hardy, quick-maturing crops and, being generally more tolerant of poor soils than onions, are easier to grow. Shallots store well, and are particularly useful at filling the gap between the last stored onions and first fresh crops.

'Shallots can be raised from sets or from seed, but this is a long and time-consuming process. Mike grows all his shallots from sets and aims to get them in the ground from mid-February to March. 'Traditional gardening lore has it that shallots should be planted on the shortest day and harvested on the longest – but this is not always practical,' he says.

Shallots are suited to the same growing conditions as onions sets and are planted in exactly the same way (see above). Each individual set planted will produce about five to seven shallots on the surface of the soil, and these can be harvested in June or July when the foliage begins to dry. Gently fork out the whole clump and allow it to dry for a couple of days on a frame of wire netting. Store as for bulb onions – with any luck they will keep until Christmas.

1

2

1 Mike favours Delvad shallots, which have a good flavour and store well. 2 Trim off the top growth and use them as spring onions. 3 Unlike onions, each individual plant will produce about five to seven shallots on the soil's surface. To harvest them, gently fork out the entire clump and set it on a wire frame to dry out in the sunshine for a couple of days. 4 Shallots have a mild, delicate taste and store particularly well.

3

4

fruiting vegetables

Mike grows a range of fruiting vegetables
including tomatoes, peppers, aubergines and
members of the cucurbitaceae family, such as
cucumbers, courgettes, pumpkins and melons.

OPPOSITE Tomatoes need regular attention, including regular
watering and feeding, but home grown fruits are far tastier
than those bought in shops. Mike grows all sorts, including
plum, striped, green and even white.

fruiting vegetables

TOMATOES *Lycopersicon esculentum*

Originally from South America, tomatoes were brought to Europe in around 1523, but it was a long time before they were accepted as a food stuff. Rumour had it that they were poisonous – probably because of their bright colour – and in fact the leaves and stems are. Today they are used in a wide variety of dishes, both cooked and raw, and contain vitamins C and A, potassium and iron. Tomatoes are tender perennials grown as annuals that thrive on long, hot, sunny days, adequate moisture and rich soil. In cultivation, they need regular attention but you will be rewarded with tomatoes far tastier than their shop-bought alternative.

Most varieties can be grown both indoors and outdoors in sheltered conditions (despite what it says on the seed packet). However, outdoor-grown plants are vulnerable to the vagaries of the weather, so tomatoes are primarily regarded as glasshouse plants. Mike grows over 50 different varieties of tomato in the walled kitchen garden and unheated glasshouse at Audley End. 'There's a tomato out there to suit pretty much every taste,' he says. 'We grow all sorts – plum, striped, green and even white.'

Tomatoes have two types of growing habit: 'indeterminate' and 'determinate'. Determinates form a low sprawling bush and are best grown outdoors, while indeterminates have a main stem with smaller branches and are suitable for growing both in a glasshouse and outdoors. To maximize space, indeterminates are generally encouraged to grow vertically as 'cordons'.

INDOOR TOMATOES

Mike starts off indoor tomatoes in early February and gauges six to eight weeks between sowing and planting out. He sows fresh seed into trays of moistened, seed compost, spacing seeds 2.5cm (1in) apart, then covers them lightly with compost. Mike uses a propagator and keeps trays out of direct sunlight until germination has

taken place, usually within ten days, and then moves trays to a warm position with good light. The ideal germination temperature is about 20°C (68°F). Mike transplants seedlings into 9cm (3½in) pots filled with general-purpose compost when the true leaves emerge – usually three to four weeks after sowing. Plant them fairly deeply, so that the seed leaves are just above the surface and water well.

Wait until the roots fill out the pot and the first set of flowers begin to open before moving into a slightly larger pot. 'It's good to let plants feel a bit constricted; if they are too happy they won't flower and produce fruit,' explains Mike. Plants should be ready to transplant to their final position by early April. Mike transplants as many tomatoes as he can into the soil of the glasshouse border, spacing 60cm (2ft) apart, and the remainder into 30cm (12in) pots, also spaced about 60cm (2ft) apart in neat rows inside the glasshouse. 'The benefit of growing in the soil is that you get stronger plants,' says Mike. 'With pot-grown tomatoes we generally get four to five trusses compared to 10–12 trusses on plants grown in the border. Also, pots dry out quickly and need regular watering.'

Each year Mike prepares the soil by incorporating plenty of garden compost or well-rotted manure. 'As long as your soil is in good condition, you shouldn't need to add manure every year,' says Mike. 'Be guided by the growth and only use manure as a booster. If the soil is too rich, plants grow rampantly and you end up with lots of leaves and few flowers.'

In the glasshouse, Mike trains all plants vertically and snaps off side shoots growing from the leaf joints as often as possible. This keeps the plant tidy and also helps divert all its energy into growing fruit. 'Inevitably, you

OPPOSITE Indeterminate varieties of tomatoes have a main stem with smaller branches. To maximise space, they are generally grown vertically as 'cordons', with the main stem supported by fillis twine attached to rafters overhead.

fruiting vegetables

always miss one or two, but don't worry as large side shoots are ideal to use as cuttings. They root quite easily to form single- or two-truss plants.'

Mike supports the tomatoes' upward growth by gently winding fillis twine (a natural jute twine) around the stem, then attaching it to galvanized wires fixed to the glasshouse rafters directly above the plants. A similar effect can also be achieved by placing pots against a wall and attaching the string to a nail several feet above. Make sure you keep the string fairly loose to avoid strangling the plant. Victorian gardeners would wrap the string to a butcher's hook overhead, known as a 'tomahook'. 'The beauty of using string is that when you clean up at the end of the season everything can be composted, leaving a clean growing environment for the following year. And if I'm worried about the spread of disease, I simply burn the lot,' says Mike.

Establishing a regular watering regime is crucial to the success of tomatoes (inconsistent watering leads to the tomatoes' skins splitting, as well as a condition known as blossom end rot, when a hard, dark patch appears at the base of the fruit).

Mike keeps several large containers of water inside the glasshouse. This not only keep the moisture in the atmosphere buoyant, but also allows the water to warm up before it is used to water the plants – this is less of a shock to them. Plants should be kept moist, but not sodden. He also damps down the glasshouse each morning and afternoon by splashing water about on the floors, walls and glass. 'Allow the glasshouse to dry out at midday and tap plant supports to aid pollination,' says Mike. To ensure that water reaches down to the roots Mike sinks a plant pot into the ground next to each plant.

Feeding tomato plants is also important. 'Don't feed until the first flowers have formed,' says Mike, 'then feed weekly with a high potash fertilizer such as a dedicated tomato feed or comfrey liquid.'

On hot summer days open the windows to ventilate the glasshouse. It may also be necessary to whiten out the windows to avoid scorching the plants. This should be washed off in October and is a good way of verifying that the yearly cleanup has been done thoroughly.

Harvest tomatoes as they ripen. This is usually takes place from mid-July up until October, but by this time the light levels are no longer strong enough to ripen the fruit. It is then that Mike ripens any green tomatoes by placing them in the darkness of a drawer alongside a ripe fruit, such as a banana or apple, which generates the ripening gas ethylene.

OUTDOOR TOMATOES

Mike grows both cordon and bush varieties outside in the walled kitchen garden, starting plants off using the same method for indoor cultivars. He sows early maturing cultivars in late March to early April and waits until mid-May, when all fear of frost has gone, before putting them outdoors.

Tomatoes prefer fertile, well-drained soil and should be planted in a sheltered, sunny spot: 'The sort of place you'd choose to sit a read a book,' suggests Mike. Bush varieties grow to about knee-high and branch laterally. Unlike cordon tomatoes, there's no

1 Mike begins sowing tomatoes in early February and once germination takes place he moves the seedlings to a warm position in full sun. 2 Wait until the roots fill the pot and the first flowers have begun to open before moving to a larger pot. 3 Mike transplants as many tomato plants as he can into the soil of the glasshouse border. 4 To support growth gently wind twine around the stem and attach overhead. 5 With cordon tomatoes, snap off side shoots growing in the leaf joints to divert the plant's energy into growing fruit. 6 Fruits forming. 7 Pot-grown tomatoes in the vinery 8 Pear-shaped tomatoes. 9 At the end of the season, ripen any green tomatoes by placing them in a dark place alongside a ripe piece of fruit.

need to pinch out their side shoots, although they generally benefit from being staked. Outdoor cordon tomatoes should have their growing points pinched off when they have established three to four trusses, otherwise you will encounter problems ripening all the fruit. At the end of the season, lower plants to the ground and cover with cloches to encourage ripening.

PESTS AND DISEASES

To reduce soil-borne diseases, Mike advises rotating outdoor tomatoes around the garden in the same group as potatoes but preferably not alongside them. Always use fresh potting compost and replenish glasshouse soil each year with fresh garden soil. Whitefly is the main problem affecting tomatoes and to help combat it Mike hangs yellow sticky traps in the glasshouse early in the year (February to March). 'Traps help catch some of the brood and then the beneficial insects start to take over,' he says. In April Mike releases *Encarsia formosa*, a tiny parasitic wasp and keen predator of whitefly. Red spider mites, which thrive in hot dry conditions, are also a problem, but can be combated by regularly damping down the glasshouse. Outdoor tomatoes are particularly vulnerable to blight, which usually strikes in July and August. 'Use blight-resistant varieties, and dress around plants in June with a mulch of garden compost to prevent rain splash,' advises Mike.

PEPPERS *Capsicum* spp.

Native to Central and South America, peppers were originally brought to Spain in 1493 and were gradually introduced throughout the rest of Europe. Sweet and chilli peppers derive from the same wild species and

OPPOSITE On hot summer days ventilate glass houses containing tomatoes and if necessary whiten out the windows to stop the sun scorching the leaves. Keep containers of water indoors and liberally splash around floors, walls and glass to keep moisture levels buoyant.

fruiting vegetables

both come in a range of shapes and colours. Sweet peppers are annuals whose bell-shaped fruits have a mild, sweet taste; chilli peppers are half-hardy, short-lived perennials that are grown as annuals for their small hot fruit. Both are rich in vitamin C and beta carotene. Mike warns that some people have a reaction against chillies, and even handling the seed can cause irritation to the skin and eyes, so take care. The heat in chilli peppers is caused by the alkaloid capsaicin. Habanero types contain the most and are scarily hot!

Peppers are raised in a similar way to tomatoes and do well in similar conditions. Mike sows fresh seed under glass towards the end of February into March, then pricks out into 9cm (3½in) pots. As the roots fill out, he transplants into 23cm (9in) pots and puts in their final position, either in the glasshouse or outdoors during June, spacing them 60cm (2ft) apart to allow good air circulation. 'If you grow them outside, make sure they are in a sunny, sheltered spot and preferably under the protection of a cloche,' says Mike. Peppers prefer moderately rich, moisture-retentive, free-draining soil. They appreciate more warmth than tomatoes and are less tolerant of temperature fluctuations. 'Peppers are neat, well-behaved little bushes,' says Mike, 'and are ideal for a balcony or patio.'

Mike advises feeding regularly with a high-potash fertilizer and removing the early flowers to encourage a bushier plant and better productivity. Keep soil moist and weed free and support plants if necessary. Harvest both sweet peppers and chilli peppers when fruits are a useable size, either when they are still green, or leave on the plant to ripen and become red. Peppers grown under glass should be ready to crop from June to July, and those grown outdoors a month or so later.

AUBERGINES (eggplant, brinjal) *Solanum melongena*

This short-lived, tender perennial is grown as an annual for its dramatic, glossy fruits. The dark purple-skinned

fruiting vegetables

RECOMMENDED VARIETIES
TOMATOES

INDOOR (CORDON)

Ailsa Craig: red, medium round Scottish variety with excellent flavour. **Alicante:** early, reliable, red variety with excellent flavour; medium round. **Essex Wonder:** red, medium round. **Evergreen:** green, large round. **Flamme:** orange, medium round. **Gardener's Delight:** old favourite; sweet, red cherry tomato. **Golden Sunrise:** yellow, medium round. **White Beauty:** white, large round.

OUTDOOR (BUSH)

Marmande: large, red, round and fleshy with good flavour. **Red Alert:** heavy cropper; red, small round.

OUTDOOR (FOR CONTAINER/HANGING BASKETS)

Tiny Tim, Totem, Tumbler: all of these are red, small round varieties.

FOR DRYING

Principe Borghese: red, medium round.

CHILLI PEPPERS

Boule de Turquie: red, cherry-size fruits. **Caribbean Red Hot:** green-red, wrinkled blunt fruits. **Early Jalapeno:** green-red, small blunt fruits. **Firecracker:** violet-orange, small pointed fruits. **Habanero:** green-orange, small wrinkled fruits. **Hungarian Hot Wax:** yellow-red, long pointed fruits.

SWEET PEPPERS

Gypsy: heavy cropper of good sized fruits. **Redskin:** early, compact variety.

AUBERGINES

Black Beauty: high yielding, good quality. **Black Enorma:** large purple fruits. **Long Purple:** dark purple fruits. **Mini Bambino:** small fruits. **Money Maker:** dependable, large purple variety. **Snowy:** white, elongated variety.

cylindrical varieties are the most usual, but aubergines are also available in white, yellow and green as well as a surprising range of shapes and sizes. Believed to be originally native to India, where they have been successfully cultivated for thousands of years, aubergines will set fruit only if given a long growing season and warm temperatures. Aubergines form lush, bushy plants with stunning vibrant purple flowers. The fruit, which is so tender that even the skin is eaten, can be puréed, stuffed, grilled, roasted, fried, curried or made into chutneys. Low in calories, aubergines contain vitamin C as well as iron, potassium and fibre.

Being tropical plants, aubergines love warm, humid conditions with a high light intensity. Unsurprisingly then, they prefer to be grown in a glasshouse or the warmest, most sheltered spot in the garden. Mike sows aubergine seed under glass from Febrary to March in the same way as tomatoes and peppers. Grow them either in pots or beds in well-drained, reasonably rich soil. When the plants reach 30-45cm (12-18in) high, pinch out the growing tip of the main stem to encourage the plants to fruit on the side shoots. 'It's hard not to be greedy, but it's best to limit plants to just four to six fruits by removing some in their embryonic state. This will ensure that you get final crop of good quality, decent-sized fruits,' recommends Mike. Once fruits are set, feed with a weak, liquid fertilizer. Keep plants weed free and moist, but not water-logged. Harvest in mid-summer when fruits are fully coloured and plump.

Aubergines have an unfortunate tendency to attract pests and they can suffer particularly from whitefly and red spider mite, but these problems can be very easily minimized by misting the plants with water during the day.

OPPOSITE Yellow varieties of tomato can be just as sweet as red ones. 'People tend to be put off by their colour, but they really are just as tasty,' says Mike.

fruiting vegetables

CUCURBITACEAE FAMILY
CUCUMBERS (OUTDOOR AND GLASSHOUSE), COURGETTES (ZUCCHINI) AND MARROWS (SUMMER SQUASH), PUMPKINS (WINTER SQUASH) AND MELONS

CUCUMBERS *Cucumis sativus*

These tender, scrambling or climbing annuals are believed to have been first cultivated in Mesopotamia around 2000BC. Early varieties were rather bitter and were served cooked in soups and stews. Today, cucumbers are invariably eaten raw in salads, although there is some debate whether they taste best with the skin on or peeled off. Cucumbers contain vitamins A and C as well as potassium. Victorian gardeners – perhaps in response to the demands of the cooks – tried to grow them as straight as possible and even had glass tubes made specifically for this purpose.

Cucumbers are divided into two main categories: indoor and outdoor. Indoor cucumbers, which have smooth skinned fruits mcsuring up to 45cm (18in) long, do best in a warm, humid atmosphere. Outdoor varieties (often referred to as ridge cucumbers) are much hardier, but fruits tend to be shorter with rougher textured skins. 'There is little difference in taste,' says Mike, 'but outdoor varieties are far simpler to grow and are more resistant to pests and diseases, so are better suited to amateur gardeners.'

OUTDOOR/RIDGE CUCUMBERS

Mike grows bush varieties of cucumber, germinating seed under glass during April, so that young plants are ready to move outdoors after the last frost, from May into June. Cucumbers take about 12 weeks from

LEFT The pumpkin patch at Audley End is an experimenting ground for many different varieties. At the end of the season it is a good idea to cut away the leaves to encourage the pumpkins to ripen in the sunshine.

1

I Start cucumber seed off indoors in pots of organic seed compost from March onwards. 2 & 3 Mike transplants seedlings to beds in the glasshouse, spacing them 1 m (3ft) apart. 4 Indoor cucumbers grow vertically as cordons and Mike uses twine attached to rafters to support them. OPPOSITE Pinch out the plant's growing tip once the main shoot reaches the ridge of the glasshouse roof – this will encourage side shoots. Then pinch out side shoots to two leaves beyond the flower.

2

3

4

sowing to cropping. 'Try to aim for continuous growth and avoid any checks in development,' he says.

Sow in 9cm (3½in) pots filled with organic seed compost, pushing the seed on its edge 6mm (¼in) below the surface. Germination is usually rapid, so there is no real advantage to sowing too early. 'Cucumbers dislike being transplanted, so it's best to sow just a couple of seeds per pot and thin out,' says Mike. 'Give them a good watering, then just let them be.'

When plants have developed two to three leaves and are good and sturdy, harden them off for a week or so before transferring them outside to an open but moderately sheltered, sunny position. Cucumbers do best in a fairly fertile, moisture-retentive, free-draining soil that has had plenty of organic matter incorporated. Remember to rotate them around the garden each year to avoid soil-borne diseases. Before planting, Mike draws soil up into a slight mound to improve drainage, then sets plants 1m (3ft) apart, making sure that the 'collar' or 'neck' (where the stem joins the root) is just above soil level, as this area is prone to rot. The cucumber family produce their roots at the soil surface so it is a good idea to mulch well. This encourages the root system to develop, as well as helping to conserve moisture and suppress weeds. When soil temperatures are above 20°C (68°F), seed can be sown in situ under the protection of fleece, cloches or inverted jam jars.

Up until flowering time, Mike and his team water cucumber plants twice a week. Once the fruit has set, however, they water freely and feed once a month with some dilute seaweed fertilizer or a tomato feed.

ABOVE Indoor cucumbers require high humidity and high temperatures to perform well. Mike grows indoor varieties as cordons, supporting plants with string and wire attached to the glasshouse rafters.

Outdoor varieties are pollinated by insects, so do not pinch out male flowers as you would do with indoor varieties. 'You may need to coax the runners to go where you want, but other than that they are pretty uncomplicated,' says Mike. Cucumbers like plenty of sunshine, but in extremely hot conditions it is worth erecting some form of temporary shade to prevent their tender delicate leaves from becoming sun-scorched.

When planting, take care not to position outdoor/ridge varieties near to modern 'all-female' varieties as the all-female types could easily become pollinated and then produce bitter fruit.

Harvest as baby cucumbers in mid-summer to early autumn, or wait until they stop lengthening and are around 20-25cm (8-10in) long.

INDOOR CUCUMBERS

Indoor cucumbers require more attention than outdoor varieties. They need high temperatures and high humidity to do well, and fluctuations in either may lead to checks in growth. To keep the plants happy, Mike maintains a temperature of around 20°C (68°F) in the glasshouse and takes care to keep the doors and windows firmly shut. He also damps down regularly to keep moisture levels buoyant. Although indoor cucumbers can be grown alongside tomatoes, they really prefer slightly different conditions so ideally they should be kept separate.

Start the cucumber seed off in pots from March onwards in exactly the same way as outdoor varieties (see p. 89-92). Transplant the seedlings into 30cm (12in) pots or prepared beds inside the glasshouse, spacing them 1m (3ft) apart. Alternatively, transplant the seedlings into grow bags, with a maximum of two plants per bag. Mike recommends punching a few holes into the bottom of the grow bags to avoid problems caused by over watering.

Old-fashioned cucumber cultivars produce both male and female flowers. Today modern 'all-female' types are available, however, even with these some of the early flowers will nevertheless be male. Female flowers are easily distinguished as they have a distinct swelling behind the petals – an embryo cucumber – whereas male flowers are simply held on thin stalks. 'Male flowers must be picked off as soon as they are recognized to stop female flowers becoming fertilized, as this leads to bitter-tasting fruit,' says Mike.

fruiting vegetables

'Indoor cucumbers grow vertically as a cordon and need to be trained. We use strings or wires attached to the glasshouse rafters, but tall canes work equally well,' says Mike. Allow the main shoot to grow to the ridge of the glasshouse before pinching out the tip. This encourages the plant to put out side shoots (along which fruits are formed) and flowers to develop. Pinch out side shoots to two leaves beyond the flower, and limit plants to one flower per side shoot. In addition to damping down, Mike also waters plants regularly. During the heat of the summer he whites out windows to prevent leaves from being scorched.

'Cucumbers are prolific producers, so expect to get 15-20 cucumbers per plant. To get a steady supply it is best to stagger sowings, so that as one plant comes to the end of its fruiting time another one takes over,' advises Mike.

PESTS AND DISEASES

The main problem experienced by indoor cucumbers is red spider mites, which thrive in hot dry conditions. Mike uses the biological control *Phytoseiulus persimilis* in the glasshouses to keep them at bay, and regularly damps down; if humidity is maintained, red spider mites should not become a problem.

Outdoor varieties are prone to mosaic virus, which causes mottled leaves, distorted growth and reduced yield. Grow resistant varieties, but if plants are affected Mike suggests removing and burning leaves.

COURGETTES (zucchini) and MARROWS (summer squash)
Cucurbita pepo

In simple terms, courgettes are baby marrows; some varieties, however, produce better quality courgettes, while some are better for marrows. These extremely tender annuals crop prolifically – producing up to 20 courgettes per plant – and are a good source of vitamins C and A, as well as calcium, iron and fibre. Courgettes

are believed to originate from the Americas, where – along with their relative the pumpkin – they have been cultivated for thousands of years.

The varieties best for courgettes tend to form a compact bush, whereas those for marrows can have either a bush or trailing habit. Fruits can be striped or speckled and, although most of them are long, tube-shapes, some are round. Courgettes are picked while the skins are still thin, and they should be used shortly after harvest as they do not store well.

Plants are prone to mildew so should be grown outside or in a well-ventilated polytunnel. For early crops, sow seed indoors in April and then plant out in May or June, after all danger of frost has passed. Later in the season, seed can be direct sown. 'In our first year at Audley End we put our first courgettes out in August and still got a decent crop,' says Mike. Plants are raised in the same way as cucumbers and do best in fertile, moisture-retentive, free-draining soil. 'Although they like to feel the warmth of the sun, a little shade won't hurt them,' says Mike.

Prepare the soil by digging a hole 60cm (2ft) in diameter and filling with a good mix of garden compost and manure, then make a small mound on top to help drainage. Space plants 1m (3ft) apart and protect from birds while still young. Mulch thickly to help suppress weeds and retain moisture.

'Courgettes and marrows are insect pollinated, but those planted early in the season may need a little help,' says Mike. Use a soft brush and move between the male and female flowers (identified in the same way as cucumbers, see p. 93) or pick a male flower, strip off the petals and brush into the centre of the female. Water regularly and use a liquid feed to maximize growth.

Courgettes are harvested when they are 10–13cm (4–5in) in length and about 4cm (1½in) in diameter; the flowers are also edible. For marrows leave a few fruits in place to reach full size.

OPPOSITE Courgettes can be sown indoors in April and are raised in the same way as cucumbers. BELOW Old-fashioned varieties of courgettes produce both male and female flowers; female flowers are recognisable by the 'embryo' courgettes set behind the petals.

fruiting vegetables

PUMPKINS (winter squash) *Cucurbita spp*

'There are many different varieties of pumpkin and squash, each with their own individual qualities with regard to shape, taste and texture,' says Mike. 'At Audley End we experiment with all sorts just for the sheer fun of it.' Not only are they delightful to look at, but pumpkins taste delicious and are a good source of phytochemicals, as well as potassium and fibre. The popular custom of carving faces into pumpkins and lighting them with candles derives from the turnip lanterns that were traditionally used in Northern Ireland at Hallowe'en to ward off witches and the walking dead.

Pumpkin seeds can either be sown in situ in May or June, or started indoors in April to May using the same method as for cucumbers (see p. 89–92). Plant them in a site sheltered from wind, and position them 2m (6½ft) apart to allow plenty of room for their sprawling growth. Dig holes about 45cm (18in) deep and 30cm (12in) in diameter, and fill with a good mix of compost and manure, building it up into a small mound.

Pumpkins are insect pollinated and, other than regular watering, need little attention. At the end of the growing season, cut away their leaves to encourage ripening, then harvest in autumn before the first hard frost. Cut the stems a few centimetres (just over an inch) above the pumpkins, then leave them to sit in the sunshine for a week or so to allow the skins to harden up. Stored in

a well-ventilated, dry spot at around 30°C (86°F), many varieties will last for several months. Traditionally, both pumpkins and marrows were grown on compost heaps as it was believed their roots would improve the quality of the compost.

MELONS *Cucumis melo*

With origins in tropical Africa and southern Asian, melons, unsurprisingly, usually prefer high temperatures and humidity to ripen successfully.

Mike favours cantaloupe varieties not only becaause of their sweet flavour, but also for their ability to grow well in the glasshouse without any additional

BELOW Start pumpkin seed off under glass in April to May, or direct sow outdoors in May or June making sure to dig plenty of compost and manure into the planting hole. OPPOSITE Plant in a sheltered spot and allow plenty of room for their sprawling growth.

cloches. Cantaloupe melons have a rough-textured, grey-green skin and sweet, orange-coloured flesh that provides an excellent source of vitamins A and C, as well as folic acid.

Mike starts melon seed off during April or May when the temperature is a minimum of 18°C (64°F), following the same method that he uses for cucumbers (see p. 89-92). A week or so before transplanting, he prepares a growing spot in the glasshouse border by digging a hole and placing an upturned seed tray in the base (to act as a soakaway, allowing water to drain freely through the holes), he then refills with a mix of garden compost and soil. Unlike other members of the Cucurbitaceae family, melons grow best in a well-firmed growing area.

When the plants have three to four proper leaves, Mike stands them in their final growing position in the glasshouse border for a couple of days. This helps them to acclimatize to their new situation, before they are dug in. Remember to keep moisture levels buoyant in the glasshouse by damping down regularly.

When the plants have five sets of true leaves, pinch out the tip to encourage the side shoots to grow, and hand pollinate by removing a male flower and using it as a brush going around the female flowers. Once the fruits have set, feed the plant monthly with dilute seaweed fertilizer or tomato fertilizer. Mike advises limiting the plant to just one melon per lateral in mid- or late

RIGHT Pumpkins are insect pollinated and apart from some regular watering, they require very little attention during the growing season.
OPPOSITE Pumpkins need three to four months of sunny weather to mature fully.

summer, leaving only the healthiest to mature. To stop the swollen fruits from falling from the plant as they ripen, Mike secures them with small nets attached to a stalk above the fruit (see p. 101).

The fruit are ready to harvest when small cracks begin to appear on the stalk. 'Check their ripeness by pressing on the top of the melon. It should give a little to the touch,' says Mike.

fruiting vegetables

RECOMMENDED VARIETIES
CUCUMBERS

OUTDOOR VARIETIES

Long Green Maraicher: excellent flavour and always non-bitter. **Marketmore:** high-yielding variety; resistant to cucumber mosaic virus. **Slice King F1:** resistant to downy and powdery mildew, gummosis and leaf spot; good both under glass and outdoors; superb flavour with crisp texture; needs some supporting. **Vert Petit de Paris:** the true small French gherkin; prolific.

GLASSHOUSE VARIETIES

Conqueror: capable of tolerating lower temperatures. **Crystal Lemon/Apple:** pale yellow round fruits with delicious white flesh; can be grown up a supporting structure.

ALL-FEMALE VARIETIES

Cumlaude: vigorous, high yielding and tolerant of powdery mildew; good for unheated glasshouses. **Passandra:** mini-cucumber with fruits 15–17cm (6–7in) long; resistant to gummosis and tolerant of powdery and downy mildew; good for cold glasshouses.

COURGETTES

Albarello di Sarzana: light-green skin mottled with yellow; good flavour and productive over a long season. **All Green Bush:** reliable, productive variety with green fruits. **Defender F1:** early variety; dark green fruits produced all summer long; resistant to cucumber mosaic virus. **Gold Bush:** bright yellow fruits with a slightly different flavour from green types. **Nero di Milan:** dark-green skin; good choice for slicing and freezing. **Partenon F1:** self-fertile variety; produces early, dark green fruits; does well under cloches. **Rondo di Nizza:** productive, round variety; good for stuffing.

MARROWS

Green Bush: good flavour; compact plants. **Long Green Trailing:** allow plenty of room to spread. **Badger Cross F1:** bush type with good flavour; resistant to cucumber mosaic virus. **Custard White:** patty pan type; creamy-white circular fruits; reputedly good for lasagne.

PUMPKINS

SUMMER AND AUTUMN USE

Atlantic Giant: very big – grow it just for fun; keeps for up to four months. **Baby Bear:** gold-orange fruit weighing up to 1.5kg (3lb); good for pies; seeds may be roasted. **Potimarron:** orange skinned; rich in vitamins; weighs up to 1.5kg (3lb). **Rouge Vif D'Etampes:** orange skin; heavily lobed fruits; good flavour.

SQUASHES

SUMMER AND AUTUMN USE OR WINTER STORAGE

Butternut: creamy flesh with versatile culinary use; stores well. **Cream of the Crop:** heart-shaped fruits, weighing up to 1.5kg (3lb); nutty flavour; semi-bush variety. **Jaspee de Vendee:** sweet-tasting fruits weighing about 1.5kg (3lb); productive; good table variety. **Turk's Turban:** predominantly ornamental but can be eaten. **Uchiki kuri:** tear-drop-shaped with bright orange skin and brilliant yellow flesh.

MELONS

Blenheim Orange: pure quality; medium/large fruits; fragrant scarlet flesh. **Hale's Best Jumbo:** early variety; oval-shaped; light orange flesh. **Pasteque à Confiture:** sweet; green flesh; red seeds; striped skin. **Sweetheart F1:** always dependable; grows indoors or outside; a good choice for beginners.

THIS PAGE Mike favours cantaloupe
varieties of melon for their delicious,
sweet flavour and ability to ripen
successfully in unheated glasshouses.
He supports the weight of the maturing
fruit with home-made cotton nets.

brassicas

Brassicas are the main source of nutritious
fresh veg from the garden during winter.
They are hardy and can overwinter safely.

brassicas

BRASSICAS

CABBAGE, BRUSSELS SPROUTS, KALE, SPROUTING BROCCOLI AND CALABRESE, AND CAULIFLOWER

Mike plants a wide selection of brassicas, including cabbage, Brussels sprouts, sprouting broccoli, calabrese and kales. 'Brassicas are the main source of nutritious fresh food from the garden during winter time,' he says. By planting in succession and in sufficient quantities, he aims to keep a good production line of fresh produce coming through the year.

Brassicas grow best in a relatively rich, moisture-retentive, free-draining soil. They prefer to sit in an open but fairly sheltered position. 'All members of the brassica family like a firmed soil. Cabbages will tolerate it being slightly loose, but Brussels sprouts like it as hard as road,' says Mike.

'When transplanting brassicas in open ground, always firm them in with your heel,' advises Mike. 'Victorian head gardeners would check that brassicas had been planted properly by taking the tip of a leaf between their forefinger and thumb and giving it a little tug. If the leaf snapped off, they were happy, but if the plant lifted out, they would sharply order the under-gardeners to replant the whole row properly.'

Birds are particularly fond of the succulent and tender young brassica leaves, so Mike and his team protect young transplants with some carefully arranged wire meshing, fine nets or one of the small 'Audley End' pots that they found on site, which have an enlarged hole in the base. Brassicas are hardy and can overwinter safely without protection from all but the most extreme conditions, in which case fleece or cloches can be used.

RIGHT Sow cabbage seed thinly in organic seed compost. Always use fresh seed and never buy in plants. Transplant to open ground when seedlings have four to six leaves.
OPPOSITE Noisette Brussels sprouts ready for transplanting.

Cabbages and Brussels sprouts have a fairly long growing season, so to make the most of the space Mike often interplants between the rows with other quick-maturing members of the brassica family, such as kohlrabi, radish and turnip.

CABBAGE *Brassica oleracea* CAPITATA GROUP

Cabbages are an ancient crop and have been cultivated for more than 4,000 years. Brought to Europe from Asia in around 600BC, the English word cabbage comes from the French *caboche*, meaning head, which refers to its rounded shape. They are hardy/half-hardy biennials grown as annuals, and are highly nutritious, containing phytochemicals, calcium, fibre and potassium, as well as vitamins C and B6.

Cabbages are divided into three categories: for spring, summer and autumn/winter harvesting, and they vary from conical-shaped, loose-leaved varieties to compact balls of dense leaves.

Spring cabbage is sown during August and September, to be harvested from mid-March onwards. Mike makes the first sowings under glass and aims to get some decent-sized plants by the end of September to mid-October. Sow seed thinly in trays of organic seed compost, then prick out the seedlings into large modules or 8cm (3in) pots. Always use fresh seed and do not buy in plants or accept those grown by friends

as soil-borne diseases are a major problem with all brassicas. 'Cabbage can be direct sown, but we advise against this method as plants are more susceptible to the vagaries of season,' says Mike.

Transplant into open ground when they have four to six leaves. Mike spaces spring cabbages 30cm (12in) apart, unless he wants to pick them in an immature state as spring greens, in which case he puts them 15cm (6in) apart and takes out every other one, allowing those remaining to heart up and fill out the space.

It is important to plant cabbages deeply as this encourages them to produce a secondary root system off the stem, which helps guard against attack by cabbage root fly. Plant with the lowest leaves sitting on the surface and firm in. Water well with dilute seaweed fertilizer, and in March to mid-April, when plants start growing again after the winter, give them an extra boost by sprinkling them with some pelleted chicken manure. During the growing season keep the area free from weeds and when you hoe mound up the soil around the base of the plants – this improves stability and encourages secondary roots. Take care to water frequently, and if plants are grown under the protection of fleece or cloche, remember to check every so often to make sure they do not dry out too much.

brassicas

Summer cabbage is sown any time from January to April and harvested from June into September. Use the same method as for spring cabbage and plant out 30cm (12in) apart. 'Summer cabbage tends to grow fairly fast, so ensure that plants don't get pot-bound as you need to keep the roots on the move,' says Mike. Autumn/winter cabbage can be sown in March or April to harvest in October or November, but Mike believes he gets a superior crop by sowing in May through to June to harvest from December into January/February. 'To my mind autumn and winter cabbages are the best of all,' he says. Plant winter cabbages 60cm (2ft) apart as they get much bigger than spring and summer varieties.

When harvesting cabbages, Mike advises cutting off and destroying the root to help prevent the spread of soil-borne diseases.

OPPOSITE Mike transplants cabbages to an open, fairly sheltered spot in moisture-retentive, free-draining soil. 1 All brassicas benefit from a firm soil, so heel the plants in well. 2 Take a tip from Victorian gardeners and check whether plants are properly planted by gently tugging at a leaf tip. 3 If it snaps off, the plants are nice and firm.

brassicas

BRUSSELS SPROUTS *Brassica oleracea* Gemmifera Group

'These are my favourite of all the brassicas,' says Mike. 'They are relatively easy to grow and you can crop them from November to March.' A spontaneous cabbage plant mutation, Brussels sprouts were first recorded in Belgium in the mid-1700s. Extremely hardy biennials, they are grown as annuals, and provide an excellent source of phytochemicals and vitamin C, as well as vitamins A and B6. They also contain folic acid, potassium and fibre.

Mike sows Brussels sprouts under glass in mid- to late February up until the end of April, employing the same method that he uses for cabbages. He starts planting out in April when they have five to six leaves.

1 Brussels sprouts are transplanted outdoors when they have five to six leaves. 2 & 3 Using upturned terracotta pots that he found on site, Mike protects tender young plants from visiting hungry birds. OPPOSITE Harvest Brussels sprouts from the bottom of the stalk upwards.

They do best in an open but protected site in rich, moisture-retentive, free-draining soil that has been well firmed. Mike takes care not to grow them in beds that have been recently manured, but before planting he sprinkles the ground with some pelleted chicken manure. Plant Brussels sprouts 1m (3ft) apart, in rows also 1m (3ft) apart. Mike and his team knock in 75-90cm- (30-36in-) tall stakes made from bamboo or hazel alongside each plant and later in the season they tie the plants to the stakes using fillis twine to prevent them swaying. 'We've found that ladybirds like parking up on the stakes as they are always looking for nooks and crevices, and it's a good way to encourage them to overwinter in the garden.'

Give new transplants a good watering then water at least once a week until they are established and growing well. As with cabbages, remember to draw up a little soil around the stem each time you hoe. 'Make sure the soil remains nice and firm to avoid loose-leaved buds known as "blowers",' says Mike.

Brussels sprouts can be harvested any time after the first frost until late March – a time traditionally known as the 'hungry gap' – and should be picked from the base of the stalk upwards. 'Don't be tempted to crop them before a frost as they need freezing temperatures to sweeten them,' says Mike.

cabbage, planting them 60–75cm (24–30in) apart, depending on the cultivar you have chosen.

Some varieties of kale are very prolific and produce virtually all of the time, while others are limited to particular periods when they are highly productive. By selecting suitable varieties you can expect to harvest produce right through from November until February or even March (later varieties of kale are said to taste better after a frost). It is a good idea to stake the taller varieties and earth up and firm their bases in autumn to avoid wind rock. Harvest kale by cutting the leaves individually from the bottom of the plant upwards.

SPROUTING BROCCOLI and CALABRESE *Brassica oleracea* Italica Group

'Sprouting broccoli is a bit of a forgotten taste,' laments Mike. 'The old gardeners loved the stuff, but as it's unsuitable for machine harvesting, it isn't grown much commercially.' Unlike ordinary broccoli, which has compact florets forming a central head (similar to that found on cauliflowers), sprouting broccoli is a cut-and-come-again crop. It produces a succession of flower heads on short separate shoots. These are particularly tasty when eaten lightly steamed and

ABOVE Use galvanised steel mesh to protect tender young brassicas from the ravages of greedy birds.

KALE (BORECOLE) *Brassica oleracea* Acephala Group

Also known as borecole, which means 'north wind cabbage', kales are extremely hardy and very easy to grow. They provide a particularly good supply of fresh, nutritious produce during winter and spring. Like cabbage, kales have been cultivated for centuries and contain phytochemicals, vitamins A and C as well as being a good source of calcium, copper, potassium and fibre. Serve kale boiled or steamed until tender, or add the leaves to hearty winter soups and stews.

Mike begins to sow kales in May to ensure that he gets a healthy harvest from November right through to April. 'The beauty of growing kale as a winter crop is that it is fairly resistant to club root,' says Mike. Sow and treat it in the same way as

served with some melted butter, a light mustard vinaigrette or even a little grated Parmesan cheese.

Sprouting broccoli is a fast-growing, relatively hardy biennial that gives a good return on the plot space allotted to it, making it an excellent winter crop. The white forms are generally considered to have a slightly better flavour but they are less productive and crop later in the season than the purple forms, which are also more hardy.

Broccoli is thought to have its origins in the eastern Mediterranean and arrived in England some time during the 18th century. It provides an excellent source of phytochemicals as well as folic acid, vitamins A, B2, B6, phosphorous, calcium, iron and fibre.

Mike sows sprouting broccoli in succession from April into June (using the same method as he applies to cabbage), and he transplants them when they have four to six leaves and are about 15cm (6in) tall. Plant the young plants in firm soil 75cm (30in) apart and stake as for Brussels sprouts. Water the plants well while they become established.

'You can tell if sprouting broccoli is happy as the centre leaves will be produced quite regularly,' says Mike. Some form of protection may be required against the worst of the cold winter weather. Harvest broccoli by cutting off the heads before the flowers open from mid-March to late April. It is important to harvest sprouting broccoli regularly to stimulate new growth.

Calabrese is similar to sprouting broccoli, but it has a large, compact central green flower head, not unlike that of a cauliflower. It is commonly seen in supermarkets and is also known as Italian broccoli, green sprouting broccoli and summer broccoli.

Sow in modules under glass in February to March to plant out under protection in a sheltered area when they are a suitable size. Harvest a little at a time in August to September; cropping encourages more shoots to develop.

CAULIFLOWER *Brassica oleracea* Botrytis Group

Cauliflowers are grown for their large immature flower heads, known as 'curds', which are generally creamy white. They can be eaten cooked or raw and are an excellent source of vitamin C, as well as vitamin B6, folic acid, fibre and potassium. Cauliflower is a cool season crop and so not suited to hot weather, although different varieties have varing degrees of hardiness. 'Cauliflowers can be a rather temperamental crop,' admits Mike. 'Unless you are an experienced gardener they are best avoided as it is difficult to get a return on the space and labour required.'

Cauliflowers do best in a fertile, humus-rich, moisture-retentive, free-draining soil in a sheltered, sunny part of the garden. Do not plant them in freshly manured land, however, as this will tend to hinder curd formation. The varieties are divided into summer, winter and autumn types, according to the season when they mature. The varieties are divided into summer, winter and autumn, according to the season in which they come to maturity.

Summer varieties are sown in mid-autumn to early spring for cropping in early to late summer; autumn varieties go in during spring for harvest in late summer to autumn; and winter types are sown in late spring and cropped in the spring and early summer of the following year. Sow seed in modules under glass about five to six weeks before hardening the seedlings off and planting them outside about 55–65cm (22–26in) apart. Cauliflowers need a long, continuous growing season and need regular watering to avoid checks in growth. 'They are totally unforgiving, and you can't allow them to dry out,' says Mike.

Heirloom varieties may need to be blanched to prevent discoloration of the heads. This is easily done by bending the leaves around the head and securing with twine or a tooth pick. Harvest when the heads have reached a good size.

brassicas

PESTS AND DISEASES

The lower leaves of cabbages and Brussels sprouts begin to rot in autumn – pick them off and compost them. Once the harvest is over, pull out the stems, remove the roots and destroy them, then put the remaining stalk at the bottom of a fresh compost heap.

Always grow brassicas from fresh seed and do not buy in plants or accept them from friends because you may unwittingly bring soil-borne diseases into the garden. Clean your tools to avoid the possibility of carrying from one patch to another.

Club root is a serious disease affecting the brassica family that results in swellings on the roots. Avoid poorly drained soil, as club root likes cold, wet, soggy conditions, and rotate the brassica patch around the garden in a minimum four-year cycle.

Control cabbage root fly by using a physical barrier. Mike cuts 15cm- (6in-) square 'collars' out of damp-proof-course material. When you cut the hole in the centre make sure that it is big enough for the plant's stalk to grow into. 'There's no point in going to all this trouble, then strangling them,' laughs Mike. Place the collar around the base of cabbages, Brussels sprouts, kale and broccoli.

Mike relies on natural predators such as lacewings, wasps, hoverfly and ladybirds to deal with whitefly and aphids. He also advises squirting leaves with plain water or an insecticidal soap.

To combat cabbage white butterfly, Mike sprays both the top and underneath of the leaves with *Bacillus thuringiensis*, a naturally occurring bacterial disease of insects. Apply when caterpillars are about 5mm (⅕in) long. There are usually two broods of butterfly: one in July to August and another in September to October. If you spot caterpillars, spray once a week, then check and spray again if necessary.

OPPOSITE Kale is extremely hardy and easy to grow. Mike sows it in May to ensure a harvest from November to April.

RECOMMENDED VARIETIES

CABBAGE

SPRING
Advantage, Flower of Spring, Offenham.

SUMMER
Derby Day, Greyhound, Jersey Wakefield, Spitfire.

AUTUMN/WINTER
January King, Christmas Drumhead, Cuor di Bue, Holsteiner Platter, Marner Large Red.

SAVOY
Best of All, Vertus.

BRUSSELS SPROUTS
Early Half Tall, Noisette, Red Bull, Seven Hills, Trafalgar.

KALE
Cottagers, Dwarf Green Curled, Nero di Toscana, Pentland Brig.

SPROUTING BROCCOLI
Purple Sprouting Early, Purple Sprouting Late, Red Arrow, White Sprouting.

CALABRESE
Corvet, Green Sprouting, Romanesco, Trixie.

CAULIFLOWER

WINTER
Armado April, Purple Cape, Vilna, Walcheren Winter.

SUMMER
All The Year Round, Nautilus.

AUTUMN
Alverde, Limelight, Minaret, White Rock.

leaves, stems & shoots

Fast-growing and highly productive florence fennel, spinach and pak choi are ideal catch-crops.

LEAVES, STEMS AND SHOOTS
FLORENCE FENNEL, PAK CHOI AND SPINACH (ORDINARY SPINACH, PERPETUAL SPINACH AND NEW ZEALAND SPINACH)

FLORENCE FENNEL
Foeniculum vulgare var. *dulce*
A native of Italy, this half-hardy annual is grown for its bulb-like, swollen basal leaf stems and feathery leaves. Fennel has a distinct aniseed flavour and contains potassium and some beta carotene. The base can be eaten raw, baked or boiled, while the leaves can be used as a herb for flavouring.

Mike sows in situ from May to July, in drills 30cm (12in) apart and 1.5cm (½in) deep, then later thins seedlings to 30cm apart. For earlier crops he warms the soil with cloches before sowing. Fennel does best in well-drained, moderately rich, moisture-retentive soil. Most importantly, it likes warm, sunny, Mediterranean conditions. Fennel is best grown without checks and does not transplant well; if stressed, it tends to run to seed. Keep the plants weed-free and water well in dry conditions. Harvest the bulbs from late September to October by cutting off at the base with a sharp knife.

PAK CHOI *Brassica rapa* Chinensis Group
This fast-growing oriental green has a mild, fresh taste and crunchy texture. The smooth, light-green leaves and broad midribs can be eaten cooked or raw. Pak choi enjoy a cooler growing season, so are best sown in June to July, with the last sowing in August. Like other oriental vegetables, it has an unfortunate tendency to bolt, particularly if subjected to high temperatures early on, and if the conditions are dry or when they are being transplanted. They prefer fertile, moisture-retentive soil in an open site, although they will tolerate some shade. Sow them in situ, either in rows or a block; space larger varieties 30cm (12in) apart, and smaller varieties 23cm (9in) apart. Keep them weed free and extremely well watered, then harvest after about eight weeks.

SPINACH
There are several plants known commonly as spinach, including ordinary spinach; perpetual spinach (also known as spinach beet, leaf beet and Swiss chard, which in turn is known as seakale beet and silver chard); and New Zealand spinach.

ORDINARY SPINACH (TRUE SPINACH) *Spinacia oleracea*
This fast-growing, moderately hardy annual is a good source of phytochemicals and vitamin A, as well as vitamin C, folic acid, iron, magnesium, potassium, B2, B6, calcium and protein. Its leaves can be harvested young and tender for use in salads or later on in the season when they are better boiled or steamed.

It is a cool weather crop and will readily bolt in high temperatures. For a continual supply, sow cultivars appropriate to each season at two-to-three-week intervals in fertile, moisture-retentive soil. Sow summer spinach from April until July, then a month later make a sowing of winter spinach for autumn use and then begin sowing again from March to May. Direct sow in drills and thin plants to 25-30cm (10-12in) apart. Keep weed free and well watered. Harvest when leaves are still young, either by cropping the whole plant or pulling off several leaves at a time. Being fast-growing it makes an ideal catch crop.

PERPETUAL SPINACH (SPINACH BEET, LEAF BEET, SWISS CHARD, SEAKALE BEET, SILVER CHARD) (*Beta vulgaris subsp. cicla*)

Native to the Mediterranean, perpetual spinach is an ancient food crop, which is closely related to beetroot. Steamed, boiled or eaten raw, it contains potassium, iron and high levels of beta carotene. Hardier and less liable to bolt than ordinary spinach, these vigorous plants have good flavour, are easy to grow and will tolerate a broader range of conditions. Sow in drills in April to May and thin to 30cm (12in) apart. Protect from birds, weed regularly and water in dry conditions. Perpetual spinach is particularly good on dry soils and under hot conditions. When plants have reached a useable size, harvest the outer leaves first and pick regularly; can be cropped for most of the year.

NEW ZEALAND SPINACH (*Tetragonia expansa*)

Introduced to England in 1771 by renowned botanist Joseph Banks, New Zealand spinach is unrelated to ordinary spinach, although it is used in much the same way. This half-hardy, trailing perennial grown as an annual has small, pointed leaves that have a mild flavour and can be used either raw in salads or cooked.

Sow under glass in April to May, then transplant it to the garden once all danger of frost has passed, spacing 45-75cm (18-30in) apart. It prefers a well-drained, moderately fertile soil in an open sunny spot, but it seems to thrive on most soils under a range of conditions. Germination can be encouraged by soaking the plant in warm water 24 hours prior to planting. Harvest from June to September, regularly picking the leaves to encourage further growth. New Zealand spinach is very productive, so do not grow too many plants.

RECOMMENDED VARIETIES
FLORENCE FENNEL

Argo: bolt resistant. Suitable for early sowings. **Romanesco:** big white bulbs with mild, aniseed flavour; sow June–July to harvest in the autumn.

PAK CHOI

China Choi: dark green leaves and thick white stems. Slow to bolt in hot weather and tolerant of frost. Sow June–August 20-30cm (8–12in) apart and harvest August–October.
Canton Dwarf: baby or squat choi, dark green crinkled leaves with short white stems. Good frost tolerance and slow to bolt in hot weather; sow June–August to harvest August–October; space them 25cm (10 in) apart.
Joi Choi: suited to northern european climate. Green leaves white stems. Slow to bolt in hot weather; sow June–August spaced 30cm (1ft) apart and harvest August–October.

ORDINARY SPINACH

Epinard Monstreaux de Viroflayí: very vigorous – a real monster; sow April–early September. **Matador:** summer spinach; slow to bolt; sow from spring to autumn; good flavour. **Giant Winter:** hardy variety; produces large, fleshy leaves; sow late spring. **Monnopa:** suitable for spring and autumn sowing; lower in oxalic acid content than other varieties. **Viroflay:** you must try! **Whale:** early maturing; round seeded variety, suitable for growing under glass both early and late in the season as well as outside during the summer; resistant to mildew.

PERPETUAL SPINACH

Erbette: not fully hardy, betraying its Italian origins; excellent flavour; use both stems and leaves.

NEW ZEALAND SPINACH

Not a true member of the spinach family. Its botanical name is *Tetragonia expansa*. Ideal for hot, dry conditions it doesn't bolt readily. It has fleshy, shield shaped leaves. Sow during March under protection and transplant outdoors from April.

perennial crops

When preparing beds for perennial crops such as asparagus, globe artichoke, rhubarb and seakale, make sure that the soil is well dug and completely free of weeds.

OPPOSITE The blanched shoots of seakale have a delicate flavour. Popular until the 1960s, it inexplicably fell from favour, and Mike is keen to see a revival. It is an easy-to-grow, nutritious winter crop and a good source of vitamin C.

perennial crops

PERENNIAL CROPS

ASPARAGUS, GLOBE ARTICHOKES, JERUSALEM
ARTICHOKES, RHUBARB AND SEAKALE

ASPARAGUS *Asparagus officinalis*

Grown for the slender, succulent young shoots that rise direct from the roots, this long-lived perennial crop will be productive for 10-20 years. Take care to choose the growing position carefully and prepare the site as well as possible by eliminating perennial weeds and incorporating plenty of organic matter. Asparagus has been cultivated for over 2,000 years and is traditionally

> 'THE BARE NAKED TENDER SHOOTS OF SPERAGE SPRING UP IN APRILL, AT WHAT TIME THEY ARE EATEN IN SALLADS; THEY FLOURE IN JUNE AND JULY, THE FRUIT IS RIPE IN SEPTEMBER.' *GERARD'S HERBAL*, 1597.

considered as a luxury crop having a short cropping season and taking up considerable space for a relatively small return. However, once established, plants need little attention and provide an excellent source of phytochemicals and folic acid as well as potassium, fibre, calcium, iron and vitamins B1, B6 and C.

Asparagus does best in rich, moisture-retentive soil in an open but fairly sheltered, sunny position. When preparing the bed ensure it is completely free of perennial weeds and incorporate plenty of well-rotted manure, compost and leaf mould into the bottom of a trench 30cm (12in) wide and 20cm (8in) deep.

Plants can be raised from seed, however it is a lengthy process as they are not productive until the third year. Mike buys three-year-old male crowns in March to April and plants out immediately, spacing 45-60cm (18-24in) apart in rows 60cm (24in) apart. Female plants (which, unlike the males, bear summer berries) produce larger individual spears but are much

less productive overall and have an annoying habit of self-seeding around the garden. 'You can get one- and two-year-old crowns, but it's better to pay a bit more and get older ones, as you can only start cutting once they are three-years-old,' explains Mike.

Traditionally, asparagus beds are raised about 15cm (6in) above the surrounding area to help drainage. Water the trench thoroughly before planting and take care not to damage the fleshy roots, which should be spread out evenly over a small mound and covered with 8cm (3in) of soil. Position in either single or double rows for ease of cutting.

Hand-weed between the rows of plants and in early February/March dress them with some manure, compost or seaweed. Water regularly during dry weather.

Allow new plants to settle in for at least a year before taking your first crop. Harvest from late April into June when the spears are about 15cm (6in) above the soil. Scrape away some soil and cut the spears with a sharp knife just below ground level, taking care not to damage either the roots or young shoots which will be at different stages of maturity. Do not harvest asparagus after July as this can weaken the subsequent crop. 'The old rule of thumb is to pick for six weeks only,' says Mike.

'The secret with asparagus is to give them enough water,' says Mike. Once harvested they go on to produce beautiful, ornamental fern-like top growth, and this can be left until autumn when it is best cut back to just above soil level.

Asparagus can suffer from asparagus beetle, which feeds on the foliage. The beetle is not unlike a ladybird larvae in appearance and is usually found lodged on the fern or in the stems. 'It's a bit of a nuisance, but doesn't actually affect the crop, so we just pick them off by hand or jet them off with insecticidal soap,' says Mike.

Globe artichokes *Cynara scolymus* Scolymus Group

Artichokes are large, highly ornamental, silver-leaved perennials reaching up to a 1.5m (5ft) tall with a spread of 90cm (3ft). Grown for their immature seedheads, which are eaten boiled, they are native to the Mediterranean and have been cultivated for hundreds of years. Bear in mind, they need a substantial amount of space for a relatively small return (expect to take no more than six to eight heads per plant), but if you have the space, they add a wonderful bit of drama to the garden.

To eat the heads, first boil, then strip off the scales by hand and dip the fleshy part at their base into some melted butter, mayonnaise or Hollandaise sauce. By stripping off the scales, you reveal the chunky 'heart' at the centre of the seed head, which is particularly delicious, but discard the hairy 'choke' that sits on top of it, as it is inedible. Artichokes are a great source of phytochemicals, and they also contain vitamin C, folic acid, magnesium, potassium and fibre. They are particularly good for the liver as they aid detoxification, and, according to ancient folklore, the artichoke has both contraceptive and aphrodisiac qualities.

Globe artichokes do best in a sunny, sheltered site in well-drained soil, which has had plenty of well-rotted manure incorporated into it prior to planting, and they can be grown from seed or from offsets. Taking offsets is considered by many gardeners to be the best option as plants can be selected for their quality and productivity, whereas seed-grown plants can be of variable quality.

Mike takes offsets in late March by using a clean sharp knife to detach young shoots with roots attached from the base of established plants. 'It's important to only work in mild weather to reduce the shock to the plants and take only three to four offsets from each mature plant,' says Mike. Plant immediately 90cm (3ft) apart and give them a good watering. 'They look a bit sad for a day or two, but they soon perk up.' Seed should be sown under protection in late winter and planted out in late spring. Alternatively, grow outside

> 'THE ARTICHOKE IS TO BE PLANTED IN A FAT AND FRUITFUL SOILE: THEY DOE LOVE WATER AND MOIST GROUND.' *GERARD'S HERBAL*, 1597

in situ in April. Weed around the base of plants regularly, and mulch with well-rotted manure each May. Cut off dead leaves at the end of the season and cover with straw or fleece over the winter months to protect from severe frosts.

Harvest in early summer to early autumn when buds are a good size and nice and fleshy, but before they begin to open. Always crop the central flower head first by cutting off with secateurs or a sharp knife, taking with it about 5cm (2in) of stem. Plants should be replaced after about three years, as they tend to become rather woody. Mike plants artichokes, strawberries and cut flowers in a three-crop rotation system to avoid the build up of pests and diseases.

Jerusalem artichokes *Helianthus tuberosus*

Jerusalem artichokes are a hardy, easily grown crop that will tolerate most soil types but prefer free draining conditions. 'Just slam them in the ground, and let them grow,' laughs Mike. The knobbly, thin-skinned tubers have a sweet, nutty flavour but they have an unfortunate reputation for causing flatulence. Jerusalem artichokes provide a significant source of vitamin B1 and iron as well as vitamins B2, B3, calcium, potassium and fibre. They can be eaten baked, steamed, or sliced thinly, raw and make excellent chips and soups. Despite its name, the Jerusalem artichoke originates from North America

perennial crops

and the word Jerusalem is thought to be a corruption of *girasole*, the Italian word for sunflower to which it is closely related. In fact, the flowers can be cut for a lovely, long-lasting display.

Plant medium to large-sized tubers (bought or saved from previous year's crop) 15cm (6in) deep, 90cm (3ft) apart, in February to March. Cut stems down to about 10cm (4in) when tops have died down in late autumn then harvest as required.

Growing up to 3m (10ft) tall and looking similar to a sunflower, these plants make good wind breaks, but the stems will cast a heavy shade, so position them accordingly. Jerusalem artichokes can grow from even the smallest piece of tuber left in the ground and tend to spread prolifically unless care is taken.

RHUBARB *Rheum x hybridum*

Grown in many gardens for its sturdy pink leaf stalks, which are primarily used for cooked desserts, rhubarb is a staple of traditional kitchen gardens. Cultivated in Europe since the 1700s, it is a good source of vitamin C, calcium and fibre, and is low in calories. The stalks have a tart juicy flavour and generally benefit from being sweetened; the leaves, which contain oxalic acid, must not be eaten because they are poisonous.

As with all perennial crops, rhubarb will occupy the land for several years, therefore it is a good idea to prepare the ground thoroughly before planting. Remove all perennial weeds from the plot, dig deeply and incorporate plenty of well-rotted manure or compost. Rhubarb develops a surprisingly large, deep root system and does best in a rich, moisture-retentive, free-draining soil and prefers slight shade. In fact, it is hard to grow in hot climates.

Rhubarb can be propagated from seed but quality is unreliable and it takes up to three years before they are ready for harvest. The more common practice is to buy crowns (pieces of root with dormant buds) taken from strong, healthy plants. Mike plants new crowns in March, spacing them 95cm (38in) apart with the roots covered but the buds just appearing through the soil's surface, then he waters them generously. Rhubarb benefits from a thick mulch which serves to conserve moisture and suppress weeds. When flower spikes appear, snap them off immediately to encourage the production of leaf stalks. Give the plants an occasional soaking and liquid feed, and you will be rewarded with plentiful, good-sized stems.

Allow rhubarb to grow for one year before taking your first harvest. Frost greatly improves rhubarb, making it sweeter and more tender. When the leaves are fully developed and the stems have reached a good size, harvest by pressing the stems outwards from the base and twisting off cleanly.

Rhubarb can be forced and blanched for an early out-of-season supply of particularly sweet stems. This technique was inadvertently discovered in 1817 at the Chelsea Physic Garden in London when some crowns were accidentally covered whilst a ditch was being cleared. 'Forcing was a popular technique employed by Victorian head gardeners as a way of keeping their employers happy all year round,' explains Mike.

The earliest rhubarb crops are obtained by forcing indoors; later ones by forcing plants in situ. However, both techniques exhaust the rhubarb and so render them worthless, which is why, traditionally, they were considered an expensive crop. To force indoors, lift rhubarb (at least two-years-old) out of the ground in November and leave exposed to frost for a week or so to break their period of dormancy. Pack in moist soil in a cool, dark spot under protection. When required, move them to the warmth of a shed or glasshouse and exclude all daylight by covering them completely.

OPPOSITE Traditional terracotta rhubarb forcers are used to exclude light and encourage the growth of tender sweet stems early in the season. Rhubarb does best in a shady spot with rich, moisture-retentive, free draining soil.

perennial crops

Blanched sticks should be ready for harvest in four to five weeks. For forcing outdoors, cover the plants in situ with an inverted barrel or bin, then harvest after five to six weeks. Rhubarb that has been forced outdoors may recover if it is rested for a couple of years.

SEAKALE *Crambe maritima*

Seakale can be found growing wild on the seashores of northern europe, the Baltic and the Black sea. It has been cultivated for many years for its blanched,

BELOW Mike uses traditional forcing pots to blanch seakale, however, an equivalent size large bucket or pot can be used to achieve the same effect. Pack with fresh manure or straw to generate heat and aid growth.

tender, ivory-coloured shoots (leaf-stalks), which have a delicate flavour and provide an excellent source of vitamin C. Blanched shoots are best eaten fresh and can be boiled or steamed until tender. They are delicious served as a gratinee with béchamel sauce or melted butter and lemon. 'This was a fairly popular crop up until the 1960s, but inexplicably seems to have fallen out of fashion and is rarely grown today,' says Mike. 'I'd love it to see it have a revival.'

Many Victorian gardeners grew seakale on a large scale as a substitute for asparagus during the winter months. Although it gained a reputation for being labour-intensive, it is easy to grow and well worth the small effort involved with blanching. It's worth noting that in its natural state, grown exposed to the light, seakale is extremely bitter and inedible.

It is possible to successfully grow seakale from seed sown outdoors in shallow drills in April, but plants tend to be slow to germinate and take several years to reach a large enough size to blanch. For

quicker results, seakale is usually grown from root cuttings (known as 'thongs') bought from a nursery or taken in autumn from older plants that have been lifted ready to force.

Seakale grows to about 90cm (3ft) tall and forms a beautiful rosette of wavy-edged, thick, glaucous-green leaves with a mass of white, sweet-scented flowers during the summer months. Plants die back during the winter months and this is the ideal time to take cuttings. Be sure to select healthy, unblemished, fleshy side-roots that are as thick as a finger and 10–15cm (4–6in) long and cut away from the main plant with a clean, sharp knife. Cut the top ends squarely and the bottom at a slant so that you can remember which way round they should be inserted into the soil. Store the root cuttings in damp sand until early March and before planting rub off all but the strongest single bud. They should be planted vertically in rich, deeply dug, free-draining, light soil, 50cm (20in) apart, with the top 3cm (1¼in) below the surface. Seakale prefers an open, sunny position and being extremely hardy it is well adapted to cope with even the windiest site. Ideally, prepare the ground the winter prior to planting by digging in well-rotted manure and in the case of heavy soils, add some horticultural grit. During the growing season, remove any flower stems, keep the ground free of weeds and water during dry spells. Plants also benefit from an occasional feed with dilute liquid seaweed fertiliser. Although new plants can be harvested if necessary at the end of the first year, it is better to wait until the second year when they have built up their strength.

In autumn, cut back the dying foliage, then in November place forcing pots or buckets over the top of each plant with fresh manure, straw or leaf mould packed around them to help generate a little heat. Harvest the blanched stems from around late winter up until spring. In May, after forcing, Mike allows plants to grow on and build up their strength for the following season.

To force and blanch indoors over the winter months, Mike carefully lifts the crowns with a fork in November, trimming off any side roots (and taking cuttings if required). He then puts the main root in a large pot containing moist, rich soil and covers it with another pot of the same size, making sure to cover the base hole, usually with a piece of broken pottery, to exclude all light. Absolute darkness is essential, otherwise plants become bitter and inedible. Mike keeps pots inside in a frost-free place and harvests after five to six weeks.

Seakale is ready to harvest when the pale stems reach 8–20cm (3–8in) high. Use a clean, sharp knife and make sure to cut away a small portion of the woody crown. It is not necessary to cut down the whole plant when harvesting; the largest outer stems can be trimmed off first and the inner ones left to grow a little longer. Exhausted crowns are of no further use after harvest and should be composted.

RECOMMENDED VARIETIES
ASPARAGUS
Connover's Colossal: early, heavy-cropping variety
Franklim: heavy cropper, produces thick spears

GLOBE ARTICHOKES
Green Globe: produces thick, fleshy scales
Violetta di Chioggia: purple-headed variety
Vert de Laon: superb flavour

JERUSALEM ARTICHOKES
Fuseau: long tubers that are smoother than other varieties
Red: good flavour

RHUBARB
Prince Albert: heritage variety, early, lovely flavour
Stockbridge Arrow: heavy yield, long season

SEA KALE
Lily White: heavy cropper with excellent flavour

Pear
Doyenne d'Ete
1700

fruit trees in pots

Growing fruit trees mean that you can pick fruit in peak condition and get a wider range than is available in the shops.

OPPOSITE In the fruit house Mike and his team grow a range of fruit trees in pots using a technique devised in the 1800s. It is an excellent way of growing fruit trees in small spaces and if you move house the pots are easy to take with you.

fruit trees in pots

FRUIT TREES IN POTS

Mike highly recommends growing fruit trees in the kitchen garden: 'It's not only great fun but it also means that you can pick fruit in peak condition and get varieties that are no longer available in shops.' For those with limited space, growing fruit trees in pots is the perfect solution. 'You just have to be prepared to check the root system a couple of times during the growing season. The trees will be good for ten years or so, and if you move house, you can easily take them with you.'

Mike grows figs, peaches, nectarines and apricots in the fruit house, using a technique devised and perfected by the Rivers family in the 1800s. 'The Rivers' name was synonymous with fruit growing,' says Mike. 'They discovered that trees grown in pots will always attempt to put down roots into any soil beneath them and that when the roots are cut, rather than being set back the plants produce a fresh, more fibrous root system and this can be used to the advantage of the gardener.'

At Audley End the fruit are grown on vigorous root stock, just as the Victorians did, whereas most fruit trees today are grown on dwarfing root stock to limit their growth in the garden. The disadvantage of growing on dwarfing root stock is that the plants tend to be weak and in need of support. By growing fruit trees in pots their growth is naturally inhibited, so stronger, vigorous plants can be used.

GROWING TECHNIQUES

Fruit trees grown in pots can be started in two ways: either buy a one-year-old (known as a maiden) bare-root specimen, or a container-grown tree (although this is the only time Mike recommends buying container-grown trees). 'Maiden trees grow fairly quickly and you can control the shape of their growth by pinch pruning and training growth from day one. Ideally, you want to end up with a pyramid-shaped tree that is 60-90cm (24-36in) wide at the bottom and 15cm (6in) wide at the top,' says Mike.

When buying container-grown plants, choose a one- or two-year-old specimen that will grow into the required shape (ideally with a strong central leader from which branches can be trained).

Mike pots up fruit trees in a 50:50 combination of organic compost mixed with garden soil or John Innes No3 compost. 'Soil gives the pot weight and stability, and encourages a solid tree,' he explains. Mike recommends using 30cm (12in) containers with a 10-15cm (4-6in) hole – 'big enough to put your fist through' – in the base.

Once young trees are established, Mike sets them 45-60cm (18-24in) apart on a bed of soil (which is at least 30cm/12in) deep) where they can put down their roots into the soil. During the growing season Mike

LEFT Peaches, apricots and nectarines perform particularly well under glass. Generally they form fruits by June which should be ready to harvest fo July to August. Look for plants with a strong central leader from which branches can then be trained into the desired shape. OPPOSITE Flat China peaches perform particularly well under glass.

fruit trees in pots

checks beneath each pot, maybe once or twice, and trims back any roots that are growing into the soil beneath to restrict growth.

Most fruit trees will flower and start to fruit from the third year onwards, but Mike advises a little patience. 'Young trees have a lot of vigour and often throw out lots of fruit. But early on it's better to reduce the yield as much as possible – leaving only about half a dozen fruits – and the tree will benefit from this in the long term,' he says.

Fruit trees under glass usually flower from mid-February to April, fruits form by June and should be ready for harvest from July into August.

PEACHES, APRICOTS AND NECTARINES

The Rivers' technique for growing fruit trees indoors in pots works equally well for most fruit trees, but for those that do best under glass, such as peaches, apricots, nectarines and figs it is a particularly good option.

Young trees should be pinch pruned early in the year once the fruit has begun to develop, with the aim of establishing a good branch framework. Wait until the branches at the bottom of the tree are 45cm (18in) long before pinching out the tips using your finger and thumb, then gradually work up the tree.

BELOW Fruit trees grown under glass tend to flower from mid-February to April. OPPOSITE Mike uses a soft haired brush to pollinate peach, apricot and nectarine trees, which blossom early in the season when there are still few active pollinating insects around.

1 Flat China peach. 2 Mike thins out peaches, aiming for a good quality fruit every 15cm (6in). 3 Thinning is carried out in two stages: fruit are first thinned out when they reach the size of a hazelnut and again when they are walnut-sized. 4 It is far better to get a few high quality fruits, than several poor specimens. 5 Allow fruits to swell and their flesh to become tender before harvesting.

'Bear in mind that winter pruning encourages growth, whereas summer pruning creates fruit. If you want to speed up a tree's growth, wait until the leaves drop then cut back the branches by one third of the current season's growth,' advises Mike. When pruning always try to ensure branches are well spaced out, so that air can circulate freely to prevent mildew.

Stone fruits, including peaches, nectarines and apricots, produce fruit on wood grown in the previous season. Each year at the base of the fruiting shoots a new young shoot is produced and this should be trained in and the growing tip pinched out when it has reached about 15cm (6in) long. Older wood is clearly recognizable as it is darker and tougher, whereas new growth is green.

Peach, apricot and nectarine blossom opens early in the year when there are few pollinating insects around so Mike hand pollinates by 'tickling' the open flowers. 'The Victorians often used a rabbit's tail, but a soft cosmetic brush works just as well,' says Mike. 'I've drilled a hole in the handle so it can be fixed on to a bamboo stick long enough to reach the tops of the trees.' Mike and his team gently brush the blossoms of each tree, repeating the process over seven to ten days. 'You'll know that pollination has been successful as the petals start to drop fairly quickly,' he says. Mike opens up the side windows of the fruit house for ventilation when temperatures reach 15-18°C (60-65°F).

During the growing season, feed plants steadily by watering them once a week using dilute seaweed fertilizer or a high potash fertilizer such as that used to feed tomatoes. Although it is not necessary to repot plants each year, it is a good idea to freshen up the pot's contents. Each February, as the tree moves from its dormant winter period into new growth, Mike loosens and removes the 3cm (1½in) or so of filling from the top of the pot and replenishes it (see p. 126 for his compost mix). After leaf fall, remember to give the pots a good soak and then leave them until spring.

fruit trees in pots

To obtain healthy, good-sized fruit Mike and his team steadily thin out fruitlets over the growing season, carrying out the task in two stages. First, when the fruit reach the size of a hazelnut, remove those growing in awkward positions. Then when fruit reach the size of a walnut thin them again to allow for their final growing positions. Gently twist off the fruit, leaving those that are healthiest and growing in the best positions. 'With apricots Mike aims for a fruit every 15cm (6in) apart, but with peaches and nectarines, he leaves a maximum of one or two fruits per branch. 'After all the work involved it's far better to get one good fruit than several poor specimens,' says Mike. To help support peaches as they swell and become heavy he uses small, netted cotton bags loosely attached to the branch above the fruit. Fruits are ready to harvest when they have stopped swelling and the flesh feels tender.

FIGS

Although figs will do well outdoors, they produce a heavier crop when grown under glass and particularly benefit from a restricted root run. In March to April Mike cuts out any dead wood and removes the tips of young shoots. When pruning he tries to create a main framework with strong sub-lateral fruit-bearing branches. Mike prunes established trees in mid-June, pinching out the tips of new season's growth when they have grown five sets of leaves to encourage new fruiting shoots. When the leaves start to drop in September he thins out the fruit, leaving only embryo figs about the size of a pea. These will develop and be ready to pick the following year. Harvest figs when the fruit hangs downwards and is soft to the touch.

PESTS AND DISEASES

Red spider mite is the biggest problem suffered by fruit grown indoors, causing mottling of the leaves and early defoliation. However, spider mite cannot tolerate high humidity, so to keep them at bay Mike damps down the

THIS PAGE Most fruit trees will flower and start to set fruit from the third year onwards.
OPPOSITE Traditionally, gardeners used small cotton nets to support fruits as they swell and increase in weight.

fruit trees in pots

fruit house both morning and afternoon from February all through the growing season. 'It's important to have a regular watering regime to keep the moisture in the atmosphere buoyant,' he explains. Mike also releases *Phytoseiulus persimilis*, a predatory mite, as a form of biological pest control. 'These work most effectively if you build up their presence each year,' he says.

From around May to June, Mike also introduces the parasitic wasp *Encarsia formosa* and *Aphidius* control whitefly and aphids respectively. Fruit trees can also tend to suffer from scale insects, which form small, soft waxy blobs that harden into a black residue on branches early in the season. Mike advises crushing them with the back of a penknife and removing by hand.

Peach leaf curl can pose a serious problem for outdoor-grown peaches, apricots and nectarines. Mike advises combating this rain-borne problem by using large wooden frames covered in polythene to protect trees from January through to early April.

RECOMMENDED VARIETIES
PEACHES

Alexandra Noblesse: White, juicy flesh with excellent flavour. Its large creamy fruits show red spotting on the sunny side and are ready in August. Best grown under glass, they are a good variety for forcing.

Bellegarde: Large red fruits with white flesh. Ready in September. A good choice for growing under glass and outdoors against a south- or west-facing wall.

Flat China: Pale yellow fruits with red colouring on sunny side, ready in September. Pale yellow flesh, sweet and juicy. Unusual flattened fruits that look a little like doughnuts. Best under glass also good for pot work and formal training.

NECTARINES

Early Gem: Vigorous and productive. A 'freestone' cultivar. Yellow flesh with good flavour. Purple round fruits that are ready in late June. Grow under glass or outdoors against a south-facing wall.

Lord Napier: Vigorous, productive. A 'freestone' cultivar. White flesh with good flavour. Red fruits that are ready August. A good choice for growing under glass and probably the best for outdoors on south wall.

Fantasia: Vigorous. A 'freestone' cultivar. Yellow flesh with good flavour. Red fruits that are ready late September. Suitable for growing in milder regions. A good choice for under glass or outdoors on south wall.

APRICOTS

Early Moor Park: A freestone variety. Yellow fruits with some flushing and red-orange, juicy flesh. The fruit are ready in August and have an excellent flavour. A good choice for a south-facing wall.

Moor Park: Vigorous and productive. A freestone variety. Red flesh that is sweet and juicy. The pale yellow fruit with some flushing are ready late August-September.

FIGS

Brown Turkey: Vigorous and productive. Red sugary flesh. Large pear shaped fruits with a purple flush that are ready during the summer. Hardy, the best selection for outdoors but also good when grown in pots for forcing.

White Marseilles: Translucent, sweet flesh. Large roundish fruits with some ribbing. Ready in summer. Grow well either under glass or in pots. Can be grown outdoors on a sheltered site. Vigorous and productive.

Violette Dauphin: Moderate growth. The large violet/purple fruit with red flesh are ready by late summer. Excellent flavour. Best grown under glass either in a border or a pot.

OPPOSITE Figs benefit from having their roots restricted so they are ideal for growing in pots. They produce a heavier crop when grown under the protection of glass.

gardening calendar

Gardening is an immediate reminder of how nature's rhythms dictate a plant's life cycle. The sun's annual transit defines the sequence of the seasons and, with the seasons, we get changes in light and heat intensity, wind, rain, wildlife and even time available to the gardener. All of these interact and play their part in a plant's cycle of growth, flowering, fruiting and decline. However, climatic and environmental changes vary from region to region as well as from year to year, so the following calendar of tasks is not meant to be used as a fixed timetable. As Mike is fond of saying: 'Always let nature be your guide.'

TO EVERYTHING THERE IS A SEASON AND
A TIME TO EVERY PURPOSE UNDER HEAVEN: A TIME TO
BE BORN AND A TIME TO DIE; A TIME TO PLANT,
AND A TIME TO PLUCK UP THAT WHICH IS PLANTED...
ECCLESIASTES 3:1–2

january

TASKS FOR JANUARY
(MID-WINTER)

Mid-winter is obviously not the best time to work in the garden, and Mike strongly advises keeping off the soil if it is frosty, sticky or wet. But in January, provided that the days are fair, it can be an excellent time to clear the land, dig over the garden and condition the soil by incorporating plenty of well-rotted manure and organic matter. Frost is a great soil conditioner, especially for those gardens that have a high proportion of clay, as it helps break clods of earth apart. After a thaw the clods can then be raked to a fine tilth.

Check and make any repairs to tools and equipment, and prepare for the gardening year ahead by setting up cloches and fleece to warm the soil. January is also the perfect time to review the previous year's successes and failures, to plan the year ahead and, most importantly, to place orders for seeds.

OUTSIDE

HARVEST Brussels sprouts, winter cabbage, Jerusalem artichokes, kale, leeks, parsnips, sprouting broccoli, swedes and Swiss chard.
SOW broad beans (such as Aquadulce Claudia and Super Aquadulce).
PLANT garlic.

UNDER GLASS

(INCLUDING CLOCHES, COLD FRAMES, UNHEATED GREENHOUSES AND POLYTUNNELS)
HARVEST witloof chicory (as forced chicons) and endive.
SOW broad beans, lettuce, maincrop onion seeds (such as Bedfordshire Champion, Golden Bear and Red Brunswick to plant out in April), peas and radish.

GENERAL TASKS

Order seeds and plan garden.
Winter-dig and apply manure and compost.
Check equipment and make necessary repairs.
Set up cloches and fleece to warm soil.
Plant fruit trees, bushes or canes.
Protect globe artichokes with a covering of straw.
Inspect stored crops and discard those that have spoiled.
Start chitting potatoes at the end of the month.
Force witloof chicory and seakale.
Blanch endive, rhubarb and seakale.

ABOVE Brassicas, such as winter cabbage, are the main source of fresh vegetables in the garden during winter.

TASKS FOR FEBRUARY (LATE WINTER)

Mid-February is the time Mike and his team start gardening again outside seriously. 'Although we get sunny days in February, it's often the coldest month of the year,' says Mike. 'The sun is still quite low in the sky and isn't that effective.' Traditionally, February is a period of preparation, because once the garden really gets started in March through to April, you can be overwhelmed with work. Some hardy vegetables, such as broad beans and garlic can be started off this month, but for many crops, sowing too early will lead to disappointment. Mike lets the weather guide him and often tests the ground with a soil thermometer (pushed 5–10cm/2–4in into the ground) first thing in the morning. When the temperature has stayed above 7°C (45°F) for at least a week he starts sowing.

OUTSIDE

HARVEST Brussels sprouts, winter cabbage, last of the Jerusalem artichokes, kale, leeks, last of the parsnips, forced seakale (late in month), sprouting broccoli and Swiss chard.

SOW broad beans, parsnips, radish.

PLANT garlic (last of the early varieties, Jerusalem artichoke, onion sets and shallots.

UNDER GLASS

HARVEST witloof chicory (as forced chicons), endive.

SOW aubergines (late in the month), beetroot, broad beans, summer cabbage, carrots, summer cauliflower, lettuce, salad onions, onion seed, round-seeded peas, sweet and chilli peppers (to be grown on under glass or outside), radish, spinach, tomatoes, turnips.

PLANT potato tubers in large pots for 'early earlies'.

GENERAL TASKS

Continue winter digging and manuring.

Apply a general fertilizer to asparagus beds.

Prepare trenches for runner beans, digging a trench about 45cm (18in) deep and gradually filling with organic matter, including annual weeds and vegetable waste.

Give greenhouses a thorough scrub both inside and out using a mild disinfectant such as Citrox.

Remove debris from around the garden to help reduce hiding places for snails and slugs.

Wash reusable pots and seed trays.

Inspect stored crops and discard those that have spoiled.

Set out potato tuber in trays to chit, the end with the most eyes facing upwards, to be planted out mid-March to April (earlies should be ready to harvest in July and August; maincrop in September and October).

Plant fruit trees and bushes, weather permitting, and mulch with well-rotted compost.

Check all the ties on trees and loosen if necessary.

BELOW Onion sets planted in spring are plump and ready to be harvested in early autumn.

march

Continue to prepare the ground for sowing by digging it over thoroughly and adding manure.

Wash reusable pots and seed trays.

Weed between perennial and overwintered crops in the open as well as under cloches.

Protect early potatoes grown under glass in pots with fleece – this will keep them warm during frosts.

Check parsnips and lift and store before they break into new growth.

Lift and divide rhubarb plants.

Continue to tidy up and remove debris from around the garden to reduce the slug population.

Use general fertilizer on overwintered crops that are beginning to break into growth.

Protect fruit trees and bushes from frost before they begin to get early bud break. Keep an eye on the weather and, if need be, protect with fleece or a screen. Start a pest-control regime as aphids usually begin to appear in March.

This is the last opportunity to plant bare root fruit trees and bushes to prevent growth being constricted.

TASKS FOR MARCH (EARLY SPRING)

Now is the time to really get up to speed with soil preparation, concentrating on getting the ground weed free and in good condition. Work over rough-dug soil, breaking down any lumps and raking to a fine tilth (if you have clay soil, do this as soon as it is workable, otherwise it will become as hard as a brick). Lightly fork in organic material spread over the surface, and dig in green manures. Complete any tree planting and order new fruit trees for planting in the autumn (suppliers often grow fruit trees in small quantities). This is a good time to feed fruit trees and bushes and top dress the rest of the garden with pelleted chicken manure.

OUTSIDE

HARVEST Brussels sprouts, winter cabbage, winter cauliflower, kale, leeks, radish, forced seakale, sprouting broccoli, Swiss chard, turnip tops.

SOW asparagus seed, early beetroot, broad beans, Brussels sprouts, summer cabbage, calabrese, early carrots, summer cauliflower, chives, corn salad, endive, late garlic, kale, early cultivars of kohlrabi, leeks, lettuce (at two-week intervals until July), onion seed, onion sets (non-heat-treated), spring onions, parsley, parsnips, early peas (wrinkled varieties) first early potatoes, radish, rocket, shallots, spinach and early turnips.

PLANT OR TRANSPLANT asparagus, Jerusalem artichoke, summer cultivars of cabbage and cauliflower, globe artichokes (end of month), autumn-sown onion seedlings, rhubarb offsets and seakale.

UNDER GLASS

SOW aubergines, beetroot, Brussels sprouts, summer cabbage, carrots, cauliflower, celeriac, self-blanching celery, endive, kale, leeks, lettuce, parsley, radish, spring onions, tomatoes.

RIGHT Begin sowing a selection of lettuce cultivars outdoors in March and continue at two-week intervals until July.

april

Tasks for April (mid-spring)

April is a time of transition: the lengthening days and warmer temperatures encourage plant growth and regeneration but gardeners are still at the mercy of sudden changes in the weather.

Continue to sow early varieties outdoors, but avoid working with wet soil; far better to wait until it has been dried by sun and wind and can be easily raked to a fine tilth. Be ready to protect young crops against adverse weather. Watch out for emerging pests and protect any seedlings against birds. Weeds also start to proliferate, competing for light, moisture and nutrients. 'Now is the time to keep the hoe moving to prevent weeds gaining the upper hand,' advises Mike.

Pay close attention to watering plants started off in the greenhouse, as new roots will be forming and should not be allowed to dry out. Mike begins to ventilate and damp down the greenhouse on warm, sunny days.

Outside

HARVEST spring cabbage, spring lettuce (sown under glass in October), spring onions (late in the month), early radish, forced seakale, and early turnips.

SOW asparagus peas, early beetroot, broad beans, broccoli, Brussels sprouts, autumn and winter cabbage, calabrese, carrots, summer cultivars of cauliflower, witloof chicory, corn salad, endive, Florence fennel, globe artichoke, Japanese onions, kale, kohlrabi, leeks, summer lettuce, parsnips, maincrop peas, radish, rhubarb, rocket, salsify and scorzonera for winter use, perpetual spinach (spinach beet), summer spinach, spring onions, Swiss chard, and early cultivars of turnips in open ground.

PLANT/TRANSPLANT asparagus crowns, Brussels sprouts (sown under glass), summer cabbage, calabrese, cauliflower, celery (early sown), globe artichoke off-sets), onion seedlings (sown in January), onion sets (try to plant last of these by end of month), second early potatoes and two weeks later maincrop potatoes and greenhouse tomatoes.

Under Glass

SOW broccoli, summer cabbage, cauliflower, outdoor cucumber, courgettes, dwarf French beans, gourds, kale, marrows, melons, pumpkins, runner beans, squashes, sweet corn, outdoor tomatoes.

General Tasks

Continue to prepare ground for sowing.

Prepare beds for tomatoes by digging over and incorporating lots of well-rotted manure and compost.

Earth up early potatoes.

Stake peas.

Towards the end of the month prepare to transplant celery by excavating a trench and putting in plenty of well-rotted manure.

Continue weeding.

Clear debris, including brassica stumps.

Remove protection from globe artichokes.

Begin mulching soil if warm.

Use general fertilizer on overwintered crops breaking into growth.

Take offsets from strongest globe artichoke plants.

Support cucumber plants grown in greenhouse and begin removing male flowers.

ABOVE Onion seedlings can be transplanted outside in April.

may

TASKS FOR MAY (LATE SPRING)

With unfurling leaves, lengthening stems and flowers bursting open all around the garden, the growing season is obviously well underway in May. This is very much a key month at Audley End as Mike aims to accomplish a good part of the work: most of the soil preparation should have been completed, the majority of the seeds will already have been sown and transplants made. 'It's really the time to care for the plants and hopefully harvest your first crops from early sowings,' says Mike.

In the glasshouse this is a good time to release biological controls and, if you are worried about scorching, apply shading. As seedlings are transplanted outside, glasshouses should begin to empty, making way for young tomato and cucumber plants.

Alongside all the new growth, pests and diseases will also become increasingly active, so step up your measures to combat them as necessary.

OUTSIDE

HARVEST beetroot, first broad beans (towards the end of the month), summer cabbage (late in the month), early carrots, kohlrabi, lettuce, spring onions, early peas, radish, summer spinach and turnips.

SOW asparagus peas, beetroot, broad beans (last sowing), dwarf French beans, runner beans, early winter and spring broccoli, autumn and winter cabbage, savoy cabbage, autumn cauliflower, calabrese, celeriac, chicory (for forcing), witloof chicory (to lift during October and force over the winter), corn salad, outdoor cucumber, endive, Florence fennel, kale (NOTE: kale 'Hungry Gap' must be sown in situ and thinned), kohlrabi (white varieties first, then purple mid-month), lettuce, marrows, pickling onions, salsify, scorzonera, spring onions,

parsnips (last sowings), maincrop peas, pumpkin, radish, rocket, summer spinach, perpetual spinach, Swiss chard, squash, sweet corn and turnips.

PLANT/TRANSPLANT When there is no longer any danger of frost transplant runner beans, broccoli, Brussels sprouts, summer, autumn and winter cabbage, summer and autumn cauliflower, celeriac, self-blanching celery, courgettes, outdoor cucumber, leeks, marrows, pumpkins, runner beans, squashes, sweet corn (protect if necessary) and, if not yet done, this is the very last opportunity for onion sets.

UNDER GLASS

SOW autumn and winter cauliflowers, courgettes, cucumber (for a late crop), kale, marrows, melons, sprouting broccoli, and sweet corn.

GENERAL TASKS

Continue to prepare the ground.
Continue weeding and clearing away any debris.
Continue to earth up early and maincrop potatoes.
Stake broad beans.
Carrot fly is active now so protect early sown crop.
Look out for pests such as blackfly, cabbage root fly and flea beetle; spray with insecticidal soap if necessary.
Erect supports for climbing runner beans.
Begin watering plants, especially those newly sown.
Thin out beetroot, carrots, lettuce, parsnip, spinach and turnip.

BELOW Sow the last broad beans, such as Green Windsor and White Windsor.

TASKS FOR JUNE (EARLY SUMMER)

With most of the hard work done and plant growth well in its stride – thanks to higher temperatures and greater light intensity – early summer is a time for gardeners to enjoy their plot and the long sunny days. 'In many ways, June is the best time of the year at in the kitchen garden,' says Mike. 'Early crops are well under way and it's the time when we really begin to reap the benefits of our hard work.' Remember to harvest your crops regularly in order to maintain a steady supply and continue to make successional sowings of quick-growing crops. Keep weeds at bay by hoeing regularly, and be sure to water during dry spells.

OUTSIDE

HARVEST broad beans, summer cabbage, early carrots, Florence fennel, kohlrabi, lettuce, perpetual spinach, spring onions, peas and early potatoes.

SOW dwarf French beans, the last of the runner beans, beetroot, carrots, cauliflower, non-hearting varieties of chicory (to harvest from August onwards), sugar loaf chicory, witloof chicory, corn salad, courgettes (last sowings), cucumber (last sowings), endive, kohlrabi (purple varieties), lettuce, marrows (last sowings), spring onions, oriental vegetables, last of the maincrop peas and an early cultivar for a possible late crop, pumpkin (last sowings), radish for autumn/winter use, rocket, perpetual spinach, last of the summer spinach, squash (last sowings), sweet corn (last sowings), Swiss chard and turnips.

ABOVE Whatever variety you choose, pumpkins musts be sown by June.

PLANT/TRANSPLANT asparagus (from seed sown earlier), broccoli, Brussels sprouts, cabbage, calabrese, cauliflower, celery, celeriac, courgettes, kale, leeks, marrows, peppers, pumpkins, squash, sweet corn and tomatoes (last opportunity).

GENERAL TASKS

Protect carrots against carrot fly.
Continue weeding, hoeing and mulching crops.
Water plants, especially those that are newly sewn and young seedlings.
Continue to earth up potatoes.
Keep clearing away garden debris to reduce risk of pests and diseases.
Stake and support plants where necessary.

july

TASKS FOR JULY (MID-SUMMER)

Mid-summer is the peak of the growing season and the garden should be at its fullest at this time of the year. Fewer jobs need doing in July than in recent months, so make sure that you find the time to relax and really enjoy the garden. However, you should still endeavour to keep your plants healthy and vigorous by maintaining a regime of weeding, watering and mulching. Pay some particular attention to the watering of plants that are in the early stages of growth, as well as those whose pods are swelling, such as broad beans, peas and French beans. Prepare a suitable place to dry and store your harvest of garlic and shallots.

OUTSIDE

HARVEST broad beans, runner beans, beetroot, summer cabbage, carrots, garlic, kohlrabi, spring onions, shallots and sweet corn.

SOW dwarf French beans (this should be the last of the sowings), beetroot, spring cabbage, carrots, autumn cauliflower, non-hearting varieties of chicory, sugar loaf chicory, corn salad, maincrop summer endive (Mike always makes his last sowing by the 9th of July) kohlrabi, last of the summer lettuce, spring onions, oriental vegetables, autumn/winter radish and mouli-type radish, rocket, perpetual spinach, Swiss chard and turnips.

TRANSPLANT complete planting of winter brassicas such as broccoli, Brussels sprouts, cabbage, calabrese, cauliflower and kale, leeks.

GENERAL TASKS

Continue to earth up potatoes.
Check and protect potato crop against potato blight.
Continue your regime of weeding, hoeing, watering and mulching crops.
Stake and support plants where necessary.
Watch out for pests such as cabbage caterpillars.
Earth up Brussels sprouts and stake where necessary.
Begin blanching endive.
Remove dead and diseased crops.
Remove side shoots from tomatoes.
Damp down glasshouse.

BELOW Regular watering is crucial to your garden during mid-summer. Pay particular attention to tender young plants.

TASKS FOR AUGUST (LATE SUMMER)

This is traditionally the holiday period and with the garden in full swing it can pretty much look after itself. Make sure to harvest crops regularly, and if you are away for a week or two, it can be a good idea to ask a neighbour to do the honours for you. 'August is the start of the main harvesting period,' says Mike. 'There's no time for sentiment, so as crops become available, get them out of the garden and into store.' When lifting maincrop onions take time to dry them properly before stringing them up. Harvest and freeze the last of the peas before they become tough and starchy. August is a good time to sow green manures.

OUTSIDE

HARVEST runner beans, aubergines, French beans, beetroot, summer cabbage, calabrese (in the middle of the month), self-blanching celery, summer cauliflower, non-hearting chicory, corn salad, garlic, kohlrabi, onions, spring onions, potatoes, shallots, perpetual spinach, sweet corn, sweet peppers and tomatoes.
SOW spring cabbage, corn salad, winter lettuce, over-wintering onions, maincrop peas, winter-hardy spring onions, winter radish, perpetual spinach, Swiss chard, winter spinach and turnips (for tops).
PLANT OUT autumn cauliflower and leeks (very last opportunity).

ABOVE Green manures, such as Italian and Hungarian rye grass, are an excellent way to help improve your soil's texture and fertility.

GENERAL TASKS

Harvest and clear the ground as you go along.
Continue weeding and hoeing your plot.
Maintain your watering regime.
Keep mulching the crops.
Check and protect potato crop against potato blight.
Continue to earth up potatoes.
Stake and support plants where necessary.
Watch out for pests such as cabbage caterpillars.
Cut away old squash and pumpkin leaves as this will help them ripen.
Start sowing green manures.
Earth up winter cauliflower and kale.

september

Cut down asparagus ferns.

Clear debris.

Harvest and clear the ground as you go.

Watch out for caterpillars on brassicas.

Remove yellowing foliage from brassicas and any Brussels sprouts that have 'blown'.

Store pumpkins and squash for winter use.

Continue hoeing and weeding.

Lift and store crops for winter use.

Make sure stakes and ties are secure.

Sow green manure.

Protect overwintering crops from slugs.

TASKS FOR SEPTEMBER
(EARLY AUTUMN)

September is a month of change in the kitchen garden. Lower temperatures at night and the shortening days will begin to slow down growth and it will become obvious that many plants have run their course. There is still plenty of harvesting to do, though, and work in the garden begins to really step up. A few heavy dews can usually be expected at this time of year and these can lead to mildew problems, so make sure that you keep the plot scrupulously clean, taking care to remove all spent crops and garden debris. It is worth making the extra effort to hoe and pull out weeds before they shed their seed, as it will save you a lot of extra work next season. Lift and put the potatoes into store, leaving them in the sunshine to harden off before placing them in hessian sacks or heavy-duty paper bags. Keep them in a dark, cool, frost-free spot.

OUTSIDE

HARVEST runner beans, French beans, beetroot, autumn cabbage, calabrese, self-blanching celery, autumn cauliflower, non-hearting chicory, courgettes, kohlrabi, onions, spring onions, marrows, potatoes, pumpkins, spinach, squash, sweet corn and tomatoes.

SOW spring cabbage (grown close together as collards), corn salad, lettuce, winter-hardy spring onions, rocket (final sowings), radish, and winter spinach.

PLANT OUT spring cabbage (sown in August) and winter lettuce.

BELOW Lift potatoes , set them down on the ground and allow them to dry thoroughly in the sunshine, before storing them in hessian or paper sacks.

TASKS FOR OCTOBER

(MID-AUTUMN)

'October is the month in which there's a marked change from the weather being kind, to being against you,' says Mike. The end of the growing season is rapidly approaching, so harvest and store as many of your crops as possible before the weather conditions start to really deteriorate. Mornings are often bright and sunny, but it is usual to have a few night frosts, especially towards the end of the month. Make sure that everything is secure and tied down, as you can expect strong winds and rain towards the end of the month. Start winter digging so that the soil can benefit from being exposed during the cold season ahead; frost helps to break down heavy soils and it also gives birds a chance to feed on soil-borne pests. 'The new gardening season really begins here,' says Mike, 'so while the weather still permits, prioritize and get on with tasks that can't wait.'

OUTSIDE

HARVEST the last of the runner beans, French beans, beetroot, autumn cabbage, drumhead cabbage, carrots, celeriac, self-blanching celery, sugar loaf chicory, non-hearting chicory, Florence fennel, pak choi, radish, salsify and scorzonera, potatoes, the last of the tomatoes to ripen artificially, and turnips.

SOW round-seeded peas to overwinter, overwintering lettuce, hardy cultivars of spring onions to grow on under cloches, the last cutting chicory (flowers may be used in salads).

PLANT OUT spring cabbage and Japanese onion sets.

GENERAL TASKS

Protect frost tender crops with mulch, cloches or fleece.
Clear debris and continue hoeing and weeding.
Lift and store crops for winter use, making clamps if necessary.
Inspect stored crops and discard those that have spoiled.

Lower outdoor tomato plants to the ground and cover with cloches to ripen.
Begin winter digging and manuring.
Excavate bean trench and begin filling with organic matter such as annual weeds.
Lift chicory for forcing.
Lift and divide rhubarb.
Cut down Jerusalem artichoke canes and dig out all tubers as they can become rather invasive.

ABOVE Roots of witloof chicory are lifted for winter forcing. Trim off any side shoots and top growth using a pair of clean, sharp secateurs.

november

TASKS FOR NOVEMBER
(LATE AUTUMN)

Lower light levels and short days are a sure sign that the year is drawing to its end. The pace of work slows down at Audley End, and bad weather conditions often mean that some jobs have to be put on hold. November is primarily a period of preparation for the year ahead and it is worth taking advantage of fine days to winter dig and tidy the garden. Begin to harvest early winter crops such as Brussels sprouts, leeks and parsnips. Make preparations to receive fruit trees and bushes ordered

earlier in the year, however, if necessary, they can be heeled in for planting later. ('Heeling in' is a term used for temporary planting, whereby a trench is dug in a convenient spot and the plant roots placed in, covered with soil and firmed. As plants are fairly dormant over the winter, they can remain like this for several weeks.) Make sowings under the protection of early peas and broad beans. This is a good time to order your new seed catalogues and to think about the range of varieties you would like next year.

OUTSIDE

HARVEST beetroot, Brussels sprouts (after a frost), autumn and early winter cabbage, carrots, celeriac, celery, corn salad, endive, kale, leeks, parsnips (after a frost) salsify and scorzonera and winter spinach.
SOW overwintering broad beans (giving them some protection), overwintering garlic and the last round-seeded peas.

GENERAL TASKS

Order seed catalogues for following year.
Protect frost tender crops with mulch, cloches or fleece.
As the land is cleared of crops, make sure to collect up and remove all debris, putting healthy material on the compost heap.
Continue hoeing and weeding, remembering to weed under cloches.
Clean glasshouse and scrub equipment.
Remove dying leaves from brassicas to avoid problems with pests and diseases.
Lift and store crops for winter use.
Inspect stored crops and discard those that have spoiled.
Begin winter digging and manuring.
Lift winter endive before danger of severe frosts and place somewhere dark to blanch.

ABOVE Mike uses glass cloches to protect tender crops from damaging winter frosts.

TASKS FOR DECEMBER
(EARLY WINTER)

With the shortened days, longer nights and onset of winter weather, most gardening activity is curtailed this month. But it is the perfect time to sit back and start making your plans for next season. Bear in mind that the key to successful gardening is to do what has to be done at the right time, or perhaps even a little in advance. Continue digging the plot and add some organic matter to the soil whenever the weather conditions permit. Keep the garden tidy and free from weeds. Most importantly, December is the time to send off for seeds, as companies work on a first-come-first-served basis. 'I like to see the parcel thudding through the door by Christmas,' says Mike.

OUTSIDE

HARVEST Brussels sprouts, winter cabbage, winter cauliflower, endive, sugar loaf chicory and leeks.
SOW overwintering broad beans and overwintering garlic.

GENERAL TASKS

Protect frost tender crops with mulch, cloches or fleece.
Continue regular hoeing and weeding, remembering to weed under cloches.
As the soil is cleared of crops tidy up all the plant debris and add any healthy material to the compost heap.
Begin winter digging and manuring. If the soil is heavy it will benefit from being left rough dug over the winter, otherwise just lightly fork the soil to ease any compaction. About a month before you intend to use the land, spread organic matter over the surface before incorporating it with the soil.

Select suitable rhubarb crowns for forcing. To achieve this the Victorians had purpose-built forcing sheds, which were simply windowless rooms, but the same effect can be achieved by covering a plant with a large flowerpot, making sure to cover the drainage hole.

Lift and store crops for winter use.
Inspect stored crops and discard those that have spoiled.
Lift winter endive before danger of severe frosts and place somewhere dark to blanch.
Set up witloof chicory for forcing.
Clean and oil tools and make any repairs to equipment.
Clean glasshouse and for those growing vines indoors, lower and prune them.
Check stakes ties on trees and make sure Brussels sprouts are well supported.

ABOVE Plan what you want to grow next season and be sure to order the seeds before the end of the month.

BIRD SCARER

Mike and his team use homemade scarers to deter birds. The movement of the shadow cast by this bird scarer looks similar to that of a bird of prey so frightens off other small birds. Take a large potato, and push in the quills of three pheasant feathers either side to represent wings, and two at one end as a tail. Insert a twist of wire through the centre of the potato. Form a frame using three pea sticks: one 2.5m (8ft) long and two sturdy sticks, each a metre (yard) long. Tie the sticks together firmly with string to make a sort of tripod with one particularly long arm. Using a further length of string, attach the potato to the long arm, taking care to make sure that it is balanced and can move freely in a swooping movement.

STORAGE CLAMP

Clamps are the traditional way to store root vegetables such as potatoes, carrots, turnips, celeriac, swedes and parsnips over the winter months. The main aim is to protect the crops by excluding damp, frost, light and decay, while allowing for some ventilation. Make sure crops are free of loose earth and have been dried in the sun for several hours. Spread 30cm (12in) of clean straw on the ground and pile the dried crop on top. Cover with a

OPPOSITE AND BELOW This home-made bird scarer is quick and easy to make and effectively protects the young plants' tender growth from attack by greedy birds.

further 30cm (12in) of straw, and at least 15cm (6in) of soil. Dig a trench around the base of the clamp (which improves drainage in wet weather), and use the soil from the trench to cover the crops. Ventilate by poking twists of straw through the top to form a flue. Firm the soil and smooth it with the back of a spade. Clamps are generally ridge-shaped to help shed rainwater, but conical clamps are suitable for smaller gardens. Crops can be removed from the clamp as required, but take care to close it up each time.

LACEWING HOTEL

Take a large, empty plastic lemonade bottle (unwashed and still coated with sugar inside) and cut off the base. Take a 2m (6½ft) length of corrugated cardboard, roll it up and secure with an elastic band or string, then insert into the bottle. Hang it up 150-180cm (5-6ft) above the ground during late summer. Over the winter months store in a shed or garage and in spring take out the cardboard and hang up to release the lacewings near the crops. 'Remember to keep predators near the prey,' says Mike.

MASON BEE NEST

Take a piece of drainpipe 10-15cm (4-6in) in diameter and 20cm (8in) long and pack with bamboo canes of the same length, making sure that the centre of each cane is about 5mm (¼in) in diameter. Hang up on a south- or south-west-facing wall at the start of the year to encourage mason bees to set up home. Mason bees are particularly useful as they pollinate early in the season.

PLANT LABELS

The plant labels used throughout the garden at Audley End are made from chestnut lath cut into 30cm- (12in-) and 45cm- (18in-) lengths. Sand them down, then coat with a matt white outdoor paint suitable for wood. Write individual plant names on in pencil before going over the letters with black waterproof pen. The bottom 10cm (4in) or so that is to be pushed into the soil is then painted with rubberized paint to help preserve against rot.

books & suppliers

BOOKS

The Amateur Gardener, AGL Hellyer (WH & L Collingridge Ltd. First published 1948. Out of print)

Back Garden Seed Saving, Sue Stickland (Eco-logic books, 2001)

Charlestone Kedding: a History of Kitchen Gardening, Susan Campbell (Ebury Press, 1996)

Collins Guide to the Pests, Diseases & Disorders of Garden Plants, Stefan Buczacki and Keith Harris (Collins, 1998)

The Complete Book of Vegetables, Herbs and Fruit, Matthew Biggs, Jekka McVicar and Bob Flowerdew (Kyle Cathie, 2002)

Compost, Clare Foster (Cassell Illustrated, 2002)

The English Gardener, William Cobbett (1833. Out of print)

Future Foods: Growing Unusual Vegetables, Simon Hickmot (Eco-logic books, 2003)

The Gardener's Assistant, Robert Thompson (1859. Out of print)

Grow your own Vegetables, Joy Larkcom (Frances Lincoln Ltd, 2002)

HDRA Encyclopedia of Organic Gardening (HDRA/Dorling Kindersley, 2001)

The Heligan Vegetable Bible, Tim Smit and Philip McMillan Browse (Cassell Illustrated, 2002)

Herbal, John Gerard (Bracken Books, 1985. First published 1597 as *The Herball or General Historie of Plantes*)

Heritage Vegetables, Sue Stickland (Gaia, 1998)

How to Grow & Produce Your Own Food, Charles Boff (Oldhams Press. Out of print)

A Little History of British Gardening, by Jenny Uglow (Chatto & Windus, 2004)

New Gardening Year: a Month by Month Guide to Success in the Garden (Reader's Digest, 2001)

The New Kitchen Garden, Anna Pavord (Dorling Kindersley, 1999)

The New Organic Grower: a Master's Manual of Tools and Techniques for the Home and Market Gardener, Eliot Coleman (Cassell, 1989)

Organic Gardening for the 21st Century, John Fedor (Frances Lincoln, 2001)

The Ornamental Kitchen Garden, Geoff Hamilton (BBC Books, 1990)

Practical Gardening and Food Production in Pictures, Richard Sudell (Oldhams Press Ltd. Out of print)

The Royal Horticultural Society: Fruit and Vegetable Gardening (Dorling Kindersley, 2002)

The Royal Horticultural Society: Pests and Diseases (Dorling Kindersley, 1997)

RHS Plant Finder (RHS/ Dorling Kindersley, 2004)

The Seed Search, Karen Platt (Karen Platt, 2002)

The Story of the Potato, Alan Wilson (Alan Wilson, 1993)

Successful Organic Gardening, Geoff Hamilton (Dorling Kindersley, 1987)

The Vegetable Garden, MM Vilmorin-Andrieux (John Murray Publishers Ltd. Out of print)

The Vegetable Garden Displayed, Joy Larkcom (RHS, 1992. Out of print)

The Vegetable Grower's Handbook, Arthur J Simons (Penguin, 1948. Out of print)

Vegetables, Roger Phillips and Martyn Rix (Pan Books, 1993)

In addition, Mike recommends any title by William Cobbett, Joy Larkcom, Geoff Hamilton or Percy Thrower.

For out of print books, try secondhand bookshops or specialist out-of-print book-finding services, such as: **Abe Books**. www.abebooks.com. **Barter Books**, Alnwick Station, Northumberland NE66 2NP. Tel 01665 604888; www.barterbooks.co.uk. **Besleys Books**, 4 Blyburgate, Beccles, Suffolk NR34 9TA. Tel 01502 715762; www.besleysbooks.demon.co.uk. **Chantrey Books** (Clare Brightman), 24 Cobnar Road, Sheffield S8 8QB. Tel 0114 274 8958; email Chantrey.24@btinternet.com

GENERAL SUPPLIERS

Audley End Kitchen Garden, Saffron Walden, Essex CB11 4JG. Tel 01799 522148

Henry Doubleday Research Association (HDRA), Ryton Organic Gardens, Coventry, Warwickshire CV8 3LG. Tel 024 7630 3517; email enquiry@hdra.org.uk; www.hdra.org.uk

English Heritage Customer Services Department, PO Box 569, Swindon SN2 24P. Tel 0870 333 1181; email customers@english-heritage.org.uk www.english-heritage.org.uk

suppliers

Royal Horticultural Society (RHS), 80 Vincent Square, London SW1P 2PE. Tel 020 7834 4333; email info@www.rhs.org.uk; www.rhs.org.uk

Soil Association, Bristol House, 40–56 Victoria Street, Bristol BS1 6BY. Tel 0117 314 5000; email info@soilassociation.org; www.soilassociation.org

National Society of Allotment and Leisure Gardeners (NSALG), O'Dell House, Hunters Road, Corby, Northants NN17 5JE. Tel 01536 266576; email natsoc@nsalg.demon.co.uk; www.nsalg.demon.co.uk

SEEDS

Association Kokopelli (formerly Terre de Semences), Ripple Farm, Crundale, nr Canterbury, Kent CT4 7EB. Tel 01227 731815; email contactus@organicseedsonline.com; www.terredesemences.com

DT Brown & Co, Bury Road, Kentford, Newmarket CB8 7PR. Tel 0845 601 4656; email webmaster@dtbrownseeds.co.uk; www.dtbrownseeds.co.uk

Chiltern Seeds, Bortree Stile, Ulverston, Cumbria LA12 7PB. Tel 01229 581137; email info@chilternseeds.co.uk; www.chilternseeds.co.uk

Samuel Dobie and Son, Long Road, Paignton, Devon TQ4 7SX. Tel 01803 696444; www.dobies.co.uk

Thomas Etty, 45 Forde Avenue, Bromley, Kent BR1 3EU. Tel 0208 466 6785; email rwarner@tometty.freeserve.co.uk; www.users.dircon.co.uk/-nfarley/thomas-etty/etty.html

Mr Fothergill's Seeds, Gazely Road, Kentford, Newmarket, Suffolk CB8 7QB. Tel 01638 552512; www.mr-fothergills.co.uk

Future Foods, Luckleigh Cottage, Hockworthy, Wellington, Somerset TA21 0NN. Tel 01398 361347; www.futurefoods.com

Halcyon Seeds, 10 Hampden Close, Chalgrove, Oxfordshire OX44 7SB. Tel 01865 890180; email richard@halcyonseeds.co.uk; www.halcyonseeds.co.uk

Heritage Seed Library, HDRA, Ryton Organic Gardens, Coventry CV8 3LG. Tel 024 7630 3517. Seeds available by membership only.

Ingegnoli. email info@ingegnoli.com; www.ingegnoli.com

EW King and Co, Monks Farm, Coggeshall Road, Kelvedon, Colchester, Essex CO5 9PG. Tel 01376 570000; email sales@kingsseeds.com; www.kingsseeds.com

SE Marshall, Wisbech, Cambridgeshire PE13 2BR. Tel 01945 583407; email info@marshalls-seeds.co.uk; www.marshalls-seeds.co.uk

The Organic Gardening Catalogue, Riverdene Business Park, Molesey Road, Hersham, Surrey KT12 4RG. Tel 01932 253666; email enquiries@chaseorganics.co.uk; www.organiccatalog.com

Seeds of Italy, 260 West Hendon Broadway, London NW9 6AG. Tel 020 8930 2516; email grow@italianingredients.com; www.seedsofitaly.sagenet.co.uk

Simpson's Seeds, The Walled Garden Nursery, Cock Road, Horningsham, Warminster, Wiltshire BA12 7NB. Tel 01985 845004.

Suffolk Herbs, Monks Farm, Coggeshall Road, Kelvedon, Essex CO5 9PG. Tel 01376 572456; email sales: suffolkherbs.com; www.suffolkherbs.com

Suttons Seeds, Woodview Road, Paignton, Devon TQ4 7NG. Tel 01803 696363; www.suttons-seeds.co.uk

Tamar Organics, Tavistock Woodlands Estate, Gulworthy, Tavistock, Devon PL19 8DE. Tel 01822 834887; email tamarorganics@aol.com; www.tamarorganics.co.uk/

Thompson & Morgan, Poplar Lane, Ipswich, Suffolk IP8 3BU. Tel 01473 688821; www.

Edwin Tucker & Sons Ltd, Tucker's Seeds, Brewery Meadow, Stonepark, Ashburton, Newton Abbot, Devon TQ13 7DG. Tel 01364 652233/ 01364 652403; www.tuckerseeds.agriplus.net; www.edwintucker.com

Unwins Seeds. Tel 01244 882 555 for list of suppliers; www.unwins-seeds.co.uk

The Vida Verde Seed Collection, 14 Southdown Avenue, Lewes, East Sussex BN7 1EL. Email info@vidaverde.co.uk; www.vidaverde.co.uk.

GARLIC

Jennifer Birch, Garfield Villa, Belle View Road, Stroud, Glos GL5 1JP. Send an sae for a catalogue of ten varieties of seed garlic. Stocks available September.

The Garlic Farm, Newchurch, Isle of Wight PO36 0NR. Tel 01983 865378; www.thegarlicfarm.co.uk

TOOLS AND SUNDRIES

RK Alliston, 173 New Kings Road, Parsons Green, London SW6 4SW and 6 Quiet Street, Bath, Somerset BA1 2JS. Tel 0845 130 5577; www.rkalliston.co.uk Fine gardenware.

suppliers

Baileys Home & Garden, The Engine Shed, Station Approach, Ross-on-Wye, Herefordshire HR9 7BW. Tel 01989 561931; email sales@baileys-home-garden.co.uk; www.baileys-home-garden.co.uk Fine new and antique gardenware.

Botanique Editions, Les Beurreries BP 37, 78810 Feucherolles, France. Tel 00 33 (0) 1 30 54 56 77. www.botaniqueeditions.com Plant labels and supports.

Clifton Nurseries Ltd, 5A, Clifton Villas, London W9 2PH. Tel 0207 289 6851; www.clifton.co.uk

Clifton Nurseries – France, 20 Avenue de la Liberte, 06360 Eze sur Mer, Nice, France. Tel 00 33 (0) 493 015381 Gardening supplies.

Crocus. www.crocus.co.uk Internet company specializing in gardening supplies.

De Wit Garden Tools. Tel 01659 50282 for suppliers Traditional garden tools hand made in Holland.

Fruit Hill Farm, Bantry, Co Cork, Rep of Ireland. Tel 00 353 (0) 27 50710; www.fruithillfarm.com Mail order suppliers for the environmentally friendly household, farm and garden.

Harrod Horticultural, Pinbush Road, Lowestoft, Suffolk NR33 7NL. Tel 01502 505300; www.harrodhorticultural.com Supplier of garden equipment. Specialists in netting and fruit cages.

Hortus Ornamenti, PO Box 62, Westbourne, Emsworth, Hampshire, PO10 8XQ. Tel 01243 374746; www.hortus-ornamenti.co.uk Fine English gardenware.

Implementations, PO Box 2568, Nuneaton, Warks CV10 9YR. Tel 0845 330 3148 or 00 44 (0) 24 7639 2497; email enquiries@implementations.co.uk; www.implementations.co.uk Copper garden tools.

Power Garden Products, 7 Bonneville Close, Allesley, Coventry CV5 9QH. Tel 01676 522257 Chase barn cloches and plant supports

Sheen Botanical Labels Ltd, Old Bakehouse Yard, Petworth Road, Haslemere, Surrey GU27 2HR. Tel 01428 656733; info@sheenbotanicallabels.co.uk; www.sheenbotanicallabels.co.uk Plant and tree labels.

Sneeboer, De Tocht 3a, 1611 HT Bovenkarspel, The Netherlands. Tel 00 31 (0) 228 511 365; email infor@sneeboer.com; www.sneeboer.com Traditional handforged stainless steel garden tools made in Holland.

Synprodo Plantpak Ltd, Burnham Road, Mundon, Maldon, Essex CM9 6NT. Tel 01621 745500; www.plantpak.co.uk Seed trays/modules.

WILDLIFE FEEDERS/NESTS

Agralan, The Old Brickyard, Ashton Keynes, Swindon, Wiltshire SN6 6QR. Tel 01285 860015; www.agralan.co.uk

Oxford Bee Company, Ark Business Centre, Gordon Road, Loughborough LE11 1JP. Tel 01509 261654; email info@oxbeeco.com; www.oxbeeco.com Mason bees' nests.

Jacobi Jayne & Company, FREEPOST 1155, Canterbury CT3 4BR. Tel 0800 0720130/ 01227 714314; www.birdon.com Nest boxes and bird feeders.

Wiggly Wigglers, Lower Blakemere Farm, Blakemere, Herefordshire HR2 9PX. Tel 0800 216990; www.wigglywigglers.co.uk Wormery specialist.

BIOLOGICAL PEST CONTROL

Agralan. See Wildlife feeders above.

Scarletts Plantcare, Biological Pest Control, Nayland Road, West Bergholt, Colchester, Essex CO6 3DH. Tel 01206 242533; www.scarletts.co.uk

SOIL ANALYSIS

West Meters Ltd, Phoenix House, London Road, Corwen, Denbighshire LL21 0DR. Tel 01490 412004; email mail@westmeters.co.uk; www.westmeters.co.uk Westminster Soil pH Testing kit.

SUPPLIERS OF FRUIT TREES

Deacon's Nursery, Moor View, Ventnor, Isle of Wight PO38 3HW. Tel 01983 840750; www.deaconsnurseryfruits.co.uk

Keepers Nursery, Gallants Court, East Farleigh, Maidstone, Kent ME15 0LE. Tel/fax: 01622 726465; email info@keepers-nursery.co.uk; www.keepers-nursery.co.uk

Reads Nursery, Hales Hall, Loddon, Norfolk NR14 6QW. Tel 01508 548395; www.readsnursery.co.uk

Thornhayes Nursery, St Andrews Wood, Dulford, Cullompton, Devon EX15 2DF. Tel 01884 266746; www.thornhayes-nursery.co.uk

Welsh Fruit Stocks, Bryngwyn, Powys, Via Kington, Hereford HR5 3QZ. Tel/fax 01497 851209; email sian@welshfruitstocks.co.uk; www.welshfruitstocks.co.uk

A

Acidic See pH.

Alkaline See pH.

Annual A plant that completes its life cycle within one year.

Aspect The direction a plant faces, often used when describing its optimum position.

B

Biennial A plant that completes its life cycle over two years.

Blanching Growing vegetables without light so that they become pale and tender. In some cases, such as chicory, it is also a means of removing bitterness.

Bolt To run to seed prematurely.

Brassicas The cabbage family, whose members include: cabbage, Brussels sprouts, kale, sprouting broccoli, calabrese, cauliflower, turnip, kohlrabi, turnips and swede.

Broadcast sow To sow seed by sprinkling thinly and evenly on the ground.

C

Calcicole A plant that prefers alkaline or limy soil.

Calcifuge Opposite of calcicole: a plant which will not tolerate alkaline conditions.

Cap A hard crust on the soil's surface.

Catch cropping A method used for intensive cultivation of crops, whereby fast-maturing crops are grown in the gap between one crop being harvested and a second longer-term crop being planted. Crops suitable for catch cropping include: radish, turnips, early carrots, kohlrabi, lettuce and turnips.

Check A halting or slowing-up of growth.

Chicons Blanched white leaf buds of chicory.

Chitting To sprout potatoes prior to planting in order to gain a few weeks' growth.

Clamp An outdoor store for root crops, using layers of straw and soil.

Cloche A transparent protective plant cover.

Coir Coconut fibre (from the outer husk of a coconut) used as an alternative to peat.

Cold frame An unheated, low structure covered with glass or plastic sheets.

Companion planting Plants specifically grown together with the intention of one benefiting the other. For example, tagetes are believed to prevent infestations of whitefly on neighbouring plants.

Compost (A) Rotted down, organic matter, usually garden and vegetable waste. **(B)** All sorts of mixes in which seed or plants can be reared or plants grown, often referred to as 'seed or potting compost'.

Cordon A branching plant restricted to one main trunk.

Cotyledon Seed leaf.

Crop rotation A system of moving growing position of plants around garden to avoid pests and diseases.

Cultivar Plant variation originated in cultivation rather than in the wild (then termed variety).

Cut-and-come-again Plants that regenerate at least once after cropping.

D

Damp down Wetting greenhouse floors and staging to reduce the temperature and to control red spider mite.

Damping off The process caused by various fungal diseases adversely affecting seedlings after germinating. Can usually be avoided by using sterilized seed compost and not watering excessively.

Dibber Garden tool for making planting holes.

Dormancy A period when plant growth appears to cease or is much reduced.

Drill A shallow furrow made in the soil usually for growing seeds.

Dressing Plant food applied in solid form to the surface of the soil over the root spread.

E

Earth up Drawing up soil around the base of a plant.

F

F1 The first generation of seed raised from the deliberate crossing between plants. They are produced from a specialized breeding programme and are unsuitable for seed saving.

glossary

Fillis Soft gardening string used for tying plants to supports.
Foliar feed Suitably formulated liquid fertilizer sprayed on to foliage.
Force Artificially speeding up plant's growth (such as seakale and chicory).
Friable Crumbly textured soil.

G

Genus Classification of living organism (the similar members of a genus being the species).
Germination The point at which a seed breaks into growth.
Green manure Practice of sowing particular crops such as rye and clover grown specifically to dig into soil to add body and nutrients.
Growing point Tip of stem where growth occurs.

H

Half-hardy Will not tolerate frost.
Harden off Acclimatizing indoor-grown plants to the outside, by gradually increasing exposure to outdoor conditions.
Hardy Capable of growing outside all year round without protection.
Haulm Stems of plants such as peas, beans and potatoes.
Heart up Stage at which certain leaf vegetables grows tight head of growth.
Heeling in Temporary planting of trees and shrubs. Usually done by digging a trench, placing in plant roots and firming in by foot.
Hybrid A cross between two varieties.

I

Indeterminate Plants where the stems can continue growing indefinitely, eg tomato (unlike determinate plants which generally terminate in a flower bud).
Insecticide Substance used specifically to kill insects.
In situ Gardening term referring to sowing seed in final growing position.

Intercropping Growing one quick-maturing crop between rows of other slower maturing crops.

J

John Innes compost Soil-based composts made to formulae developed in the 1930s by the John Innes Horticultural Institute.

L

Lateral Side growth.
Leaching Usually refers to plant food being washed out of soil by excessive rain or watering.
Leaf axil The angle between a stem and a leaf stalk.
Legumes Member of pea family.

M

Mulch Top dressing applied to soil's surface to help conserve moisture, suppress weeds and keep soil cool during summer. Material used for mulch includes well-rotted, strawy manure, grass clippings, shredded bark and compost.

O

Off-set Young plant produced asexually alongside parent.
Organic gardening A school of gardening that uses only substances naturally occurring in the garden environment.

P

Pan A hard layer under the surface of the soil that is harmful to plant growth as it is often impermeable to water and air. Digging, hoeing and forking breaks it up as does the addition of organic matter and horticultural grit.
Perennial A plant with an indefinite life cycle (or at least three seasons long).
pH Soil and potting mixtures can be either acid, alkaline or neutral. The extent to which a substance is acid or alkaline is measured on a logarithmic scale called the pH scale, with 7 being neutral, 1 being highly acidic and 10 being highly alkaline.
Pinching out Removing a plant's growing tip to discour-

age further vertical growth and encourage horizontal side shoots.

Potager An ornamental vegetable plot.

Pot on Move plants from the pot that they are growing in to a larger size pot to allow for further root development.

Predator Gardening term for various animals that feed upon unwanted garden pests. For example ladybirds feed upon aphids.

Pre-germinate/sprout Germination of seeds on damp absorbent paper prior to sowing.

Prick out A delicate operation involving the transfer of fragile young seedlings from their initial growing place to be spaced evenly in a seed tray or potted on singly.

Propagation Increasing plants by appropriate measures. Seed, cuttings, or division.

R

Radicle the first root produced by a seedling.

Raffia Strips of flat, fibrous material made from the raffia palm, used by gardeners for tying in plants.

Raised beds Plant beds raised above the ground, usually by using boards as edging. Raised beds ensure good drainage.

Recycled green waste Organic matter such as grass clippings and prunings, often available from local councils.

Root crops Crops such as parsnips, carrots and skirret, which are harvested for their edible fleshy root.

Rootstock The stock on which a tree or shrub is grafted.

S

Seedling A very young plant, recently germinated.

Side shoot Sub-lateral growth that appears in the axis of laterals.

Species A group of plants with clearly distinguishable characteristics and which breed true consistently.

Spit A spade's depth of soil, based on the average blade length of 25–30cm (10–12in).

Stem Part of plant, usually vertical, which grows above ground and gives rise to leaves, side growth and flowers.

Subsoil Layer below topsoil.

Successional sowing Staggered sowing of seeds so that crops are not all ready to harvest at the same time.

T

Tap root Strong root that grows quickly.

Tender Unable to survive frost.

Thinning Reducing number of plants growing in a particular spot to allow those remaining to have more space, light and nutrients.

Tilth Crumbly textured soil, the result of good cultivation.

Tine The prong, spike or tooth of a tool, such as a gardening fork.

Transplanting Moving a plant from one growing position to another.

Trench A furrow with steep vertical sides dug out of the soil.

Truss Compact cluster of flowers or fruits arising from a single centre.

Tuber Swollen stem or root used by plants to store food during a period of rest.

Variety A distinct variation in a wild species.

Vermiculite A light, mineral material used to increase porosity of growing mediums.

TEMPERATURE CONVERSIONS

To convert **°C into °F**: multiply by 9, divide by 5 and add 32
To convert **°F into °C**: subtract 32, multiply by 5, divide by 9

index

author's acknowledgements

My heartfelt gratitude goes to Mike Thurlow, who is an inspiring and delightful teacher. His knowledge, enthusiasm and vital input make the book what it is.

Thanks go to Gavin Kingcome for his outstanding photography, patience and good humour.

I would also like to thank my colleagues past and present at *Gardens Illustrated*, especially Clare Foster, Rosie Atkins, Hannah Attwell, Galiena Hitchman, Lisa Amphlett, Helen Bonthrone, Zoe Deleuil, Sian Lewis, Ali Bell and publisher Dominic Murray.

At Conran I'd like to thank Katey Day, Valerie Fong and Lorraine Dickey.

Last, but certainly not least, a big thank you to my friends and family, especially my ever patient son, Luke.

First published in 2005 by CONRAN OCTOPUS LIMITED, a part of Octopus Publishing Group, 2–4 Heron Quays, London E14 4JP www.conran-octopus.co.uk

Text copyright © Gardens Illustrated 2005
Photography copyright © Gardens Illustrated 2005
Illustration page 11 copyright © Antony Sidwell 2005
Design and layout copyright © Conran Octopus 2005

The right of Juliet Roberts to be identified as Author of this Work has been asserted by her in accordance with the Copyright, Designs and Patents Act 1998

PUBLISHING DIRECTOR: Lorraine Dickey
COMMISSIONING EDITOR: Katey Day
ART DIRECTOR: Chi Lam
DESIGN: Valerie Fong
PRODUCTION MANAGER: Angela Couchman
PHOTOGRAPHY: Gavin Kingcome
JACKET PORTRAIT PHOTOGRAPHY: Ali Bell

British Cataloguing-in-Publication Data.
A catalogue record for this book is available from the British Library.

ISBN 1 84091 394 0

To order please ring CONRAN OCTOPUS DIRECT on 01903 828503

PRINTED AND BOUND IN CHINA